Places to be Blessed

10-5-2006

To Peggy,
Thanks for allowing me to have my first book signing in your lovely Café. Coffee Cup is my favorite spot to hang out.
Valerie Bradley Holliday

Places to be Blessed

Valerie Bradley-Holliday Ph.D.

Copyright © 2006 by Valerie Bradley-Holliday Ph.D..

ISBN: Softcover   1-4257-1312-2

All rights reserved. No part of this book may be reproduced or transmitted in any form or by any means, electronic or mechanical, including photocopying, recording, or by any information storage and retrieval system, without permission in writing from the copyright owner.

This book was printed in the United States of America.

To order additional copies of this book, contact:
Xlibris Corporation
1-888-795-4274
www.Xlibris.com
Orders@Xlibris.com

33832

Contents

Chapter 1: Aboutness 7
Chapter 2: Situations 14
Chapter 3: Belongingness 27
Chapter 4: Affinity 35
Chapter 5: Evaluation 44
Chapter 6: Cultivation 55
Chapter 7: Conclusion 60

Chapter 1

ABOUTNESS

An African American Tale: A mermaid was captured and put with a doctor's "ungodly things." A man who worked for the doctor told this to the townspeople and also said the poor mermaid, shrinking due to her captivity, had two gold fish swimming around her. Captured, shrunken and miserable the mermaid called upon the sea to help her. This caused the townspeople to worry and demand of the doctor the release of the mermaid. One brave man even entered the doctor's home, went to the basement and saw the mermaid. In his attempt to save the mermaid, some jars were smashed releasing slithering things, which came out of the doctor's door and was witnessed by the townspeople. He described the mermaid as "beyond beautiful" and clutching the edge of the jar, begging to be set free. The townspeople fretted about what the man told them and felt sorry for the mermaid knowing her release would stop the rain. They returned with a group of people to ask the doctor to release this mer-woman. The doctor denied having any mermaid and a "tall white man" threatened "if you don't leave at once, we'll call out the army to make you leave." The rains stopped, the mermaid was never found, and the townspeople were left to clean up the muck. They still say you can smell dead fish odors on hot days (Aardema, 1995).

At the age of four, I had to come to the realization that my life would never be the same. Nothing was ever going to be the same including holding onto my childhood. The mother I knew before was all warmth, smiles and hugs. The smell of Jergen's Lotion still brings me back to my earliest memories of my mother. The last memory I have of my mother before her transformation was when she locked us in the bedroom to keep us away from my father. While he ranted outside the door, she let me play in her jewelry box and try on things. She let me venture into her closet and try on clothes. Then, the horror of drastic change came. The unreality of the mermaid folktale adapts well to my discussion of the loss of my mother. The loss of my mother was a disruption in my early social interaction process.

Early social interaction can affect adult relationships due to unrecognized anger and fear of further abandonment. The folktale is a representation of what happens when social interaction processes are disrupted both for the townspeople and the unfortunate mermaid. It reminds me of the disruption of my own social interaction processes at my earliest stages within my family. This has had lasting effects on my social identity with respect to self-concept, self-esteem, self-efficacy, self-monitoring behavior, self-focusing and gender.

The strong attachment I had with my mother was swept away by her nervous breakdown. An emotional freight train carried her away on a trip that would span over twenty-years. Even though coming physically near to us, she is never emotionally the same. Her erratic behavior almost resulted in our placement in foster care. Her diagnosis was schizophrenia and the therapy at the time included shock treatments. Her shock treatments were so intense that one time she came home and did not know who we were. It scared me to discover that my mother did not know me. I remember, five, standing in front of my mother and asking her to "please tell me who I am." I held both of her hands and she pulled away from me as if I was a stranger. My mom recognized us less and she started beating us and neglecting us. She was no longer recognizable as the mother I once knew. And my brother and I started running away and stealing which brought the attention of juvenile officers.

The entrance of the "White Man" in the mer-woman story in which he intervenes when he thinks there is going to be big trouble and enforcing his rules on the situation, are like the juvenile officers involvement in our situation. They entered our lives when there was an issue that affected the community in some way a "big problem" as perceived by them. Juvenile officers entered my life over this period of time. From the age of four to twelve, I faced the constant threat of being placed in a "foster home" and "split up" and becoming "a ward." Some words I understood at the time and some I did not. I know that I did not want the BIG WHITE MAN who picked us up to separate me from my brother. As much as, I could not stand for my mother's intense beatings (sometimes with the heel of her shoe or a hanger) or being in reach of my abusive uncle in my grandmother's home, I loved my grandmother and I loved my brother and I did not want to be separated from what I knew. So the alternative was to run and I ran with no place to run to.

I learned through these early social interactions that the value of being female, especially African American female is very low. The only point that seemed to be of any value in this early experience was what was between my legs and I could not understand why and there was no one to tell me. Because of this I became depressed and emotionally withdrawn, even when I came to know the kind counselor at one school or an interested teacher at another, as soon as I felt like I had the strength to speak up, we would just move on.

Mom could never settle down in one place after she separated from my father. When we left our mobile home in Denver, Colorado, my mom took me, four-years-old and my infant brother from the stability of home (as we knew it) to my maternal grandmother's home. Mom only took us with the clothes on our back. She did not settle down in her mom's home either. One time she woke in the middle of the night screaming that my Dad was outside of the house and threatening to kill her, shortly after that she had another nervous breakdown. My mom's emotional roller coaster and her physically taking us from place to place made me feel unmoored.

We traveled from Colorado to Illinois, back and forth, at least three trips. I looked forward to seeing my grandmother when we stayed in Illinois. But these visits also had a dark side. In these visits to my grandmother, one of my uncle's was sexually abusive and would do strange things like making me hold my hand under extremely hot or cold water, or stand for hours naked in front of the air conditioner. The worse times were when he took me to the coal bin. My grandmother had a basement that on one half was cement flooring where she had a small beauty parlor. In the other half, was the pot-bellied furnace, which you could see into. Through the grate, which looked like a mouth ready to swallow little children, you could see the flames from the now "converted to gas" furnace. They used to stoke that furnace with coal. Off of the furnace room was the coal bin. The coal bin, with its dirt floor and dark recesses seemed enormous when I was a child. My uncle made me stand naked in there. I could hear things crawling in there. I could not leave until he let me know when my time was up. I lost my spirit in there. This continued for a period of four years. While my uncle was robbing me of what remained of my childhood innocence, I was forced to face another loss.

My parents formally divorced when I was eight years old. I was brought to testify in court and I was terrified. I had to tell them about my Dad hurting my mom. My parents divorced over irreconcilable differences and my dad's wages were garnished.

Like the shrunken mermaid, each day, I diminished through this sexual abuse and mother and father loss. My uncle's ritual abuse destroyed my self-schema, and comfortable and trusting beliefs and feelings I had about the world diminished. Aside from the discontinued ability to formulate a self-concept, my self-esteem was threatened through verbal admonishments. To him, I was not good enough. I was not sexually enticing (I was a child!). I was everything undesirable. To me, I began to go numb. I began to develop an undifferentiated sexual identity that was neither strictly male nor female. My grandmother credited me later with being a tom-boy.

Even, my uncle began noticing this, calling me an "automaton." Why show expression? I became highly self-monitoring and cognitive. Inside as the personified mermaid banging on the glass jar to be released, I was screaming! The real, captured me was longing to be free. This was the time in my life when I began learning how to compartmentalize. My uncle told me not to tell anyone what was happening or "something bad would happen."

Reinforcing this was the uncertainty of the situation. I did not know where I would live or with whom. My grandmother honored "her little boy." He was the crown jewel of her achievement. The sun rose and set upon him in her eyes and he could never do anything wrong. So I could not go to her with something as terrible as his sexual mistreatment of me and be validated. My mother was gone. In place of the mother that I once knew, was a person called "mother" who beat, starved, and locked me up. I did not know where my dad was and I was not sure if he cared whether I lived or died. Perhaps, I was the cause of all my parents' discontent. Didn't my dad want his first born to be a son?

There existed a great discrepancy between my ideal self and who I really was. This gap decreased my self-esteem. I had extreme personal difficulties resulting from my parents' problem relationship, my childhood sexual abuse, and increased exposure to my abuser. As a consequence, negative self-evaluations became internalized. Years later in counseling, I discovered that these can crop up has auditory hallucinations during times of extreme stress (i.e., my uncle's voice telling me that I am stupid). I thought that I was going crazy which added to the issue of low self-esteem.

My childhood experience has had lasting effects on my own family and I. As with the "townspeople" in the tale, you can still smell the fish odor today. I have learned that this is what comes of a life built on lies. But I had hope and I begin to move beyond just a hurt person to one who helps.

I have had some positives from the experience. I became incredibly self-focused and heightened my self-monitoring behavior which, years later, helped me to be a good student. I am thankful that I did not disassociate and split into divergent selves, which can happen, with each personality having the potential not to know what the other is doing. I know that I can work a lifetime on my low self-esteem and develop new attachments to reinforce what a wonderful, beautiful person I am. But nothing can completely undo the wounds inflicted by those early years. I can however, bear the scar and wear it as a badge of honor. My life illustrates my ability to "take a stand" and overcome something so incredibly brutal to my psyche.

As evidenced by my paper entitled, "Am I angry" Search for a Comprehensive Feminist Voice," I write: "I was taught to be tough, strong, self-reliant and my grandmother reinforced these issues with an emphasis on education. Hilliard speaks on the strength and resilience apparent in Blacks and minorities despite adversity and oppression. I strongly believe that this is due to some type of mentorship. I had my grandmother and although she could not help academically she was able to access others who could, i.e., counselors, former school teachers. These early life situations prepared me in responsible ways to be a mother, a provider, and an independent thinker."

Because you see, deep down, where that "me" was hollering to be set free was my key to salvation. I also had the benefit of a very early, secure attachment to my mother. I believe that the strength of that bond carried me through some of my most difficult moments. I was able to transcend the hurt and convert my anger into a power and motivation to help others.

In my later life, I have been able to build up those aspects, which were low, through self-efficacy. My heightened self-efficacy has come as a consequence of my direct, successful, and positive academic, social and professional opportunities. I had ordinary and extraordinary social opportunities. While attending Wayne State University's Advanced Standing Master of Social Work Program, I met an African American Physicist, Virgil Jones. Dr. Jones taught at Princeton and had been Albert Einstein's neighbor. Jones spoke at the Quest for Peace Conference in 1980. The conference was entitled Conference for Peace and Conflict Studies. This was before Glasnost in the Soviet Union and set the stage for it. Dr. Jones told me 'little did I know that involving myself in such matters would have such impact.' In reply, I remembered saying something one of my undergraduate social work professors said to me: "\'We must know that the things we do and say are fateful.' My discussion with Professor Jones put me in contact with another professor on campus and my life snowballed from there. I still get this tingling feeling that this man chose to talk to me. His consideration gave me the impetus to push forth on my own in the, then, unfamiliar academic waters of Wayne State University and Detroit, Michigan as a whole. I also was encouraged to look on my past with encouragement and hope rather than despair.

I begin the process of forgiving my uncle because in forgiveness there is a certain salvation. The first step, however, is in understanding why he set out to kill my spirit. To answer that is to go for the more global question of, "Why do we try to kill each other's spirit?"

The question was both fully formed in my mind and the answer apparent in the powerful presentation given by Lani Guinier. Lani Guinier is the first African American woman to become a tenured professor at Harvard Law School and she is the author of several books, including Lift Every Voice and The Tyranny of the Majority. She gave a presentation at Michigan Technological University to deliver her message on civil rights and social justice. From her message, I learned that the rage we feel inside us comes from not having a voice anywhere. This is especially true when the stage for marginalism has already been set.

Yet, does this have to be the final story? Do we have to accept our "fate"? Like the mermaid in the story, must we disappear, never to be heard from again? No, we can come together as brothers and sisters under one roof and assist one another. I have always felt that is our responsibility.

I never wanted to be a leader, yet we all have the potential to be leaders. We can lead collaborative efforts to help one another achieve a valid and valuable education. How does this happen? It occurs through practiced engagement that helps us reenter society through our own initiatives, on our own terms and increases our ability to solve problems. Does this happen overnight? No. But we can learn to curb our natural tendency to feel anger or rage and redirect it into a positive force that can punch a hole in the status quo altering it forever.

African American Psychologist, Kenneth B. Clark (1963) suggests in his book Prejudice and Your Child that self-destructive behaviors result from social rejection. Further social rejection results from self-destructive behaviors, such as, aggression, anti-socialism, and delinquency. In order to break free of these self-destructive social behaviors, which is an understandable result of living in pathological social environment, children can be helped by directing their energy to help themselves and others in constructive ways (Clark, 1963). In light of this knowledge with the filter of my past and with my eyes to the future, I have a sense of greater purpose.

As a parent, I can address my own personal pressures in the face of racial and misogynistic pressures, by teaching my children tolerance and compassion for other human beings—even those who are prejudiced toward them. I have struggled to understand that the person who hates is a victim. The person who hates is a victim of his own cognitive distortions and ignorance (Clark, 1963). As Clark suggests if a child can be taught to understand this he or she has a cure for the poison that develops in victims of discrimination. Thus, as a consequence, we can hopefully break the cycle of social rejection, victimization, and discrimination.

To put it succinctly, I will quote a friend: "Hurt people; hurt people." In order to be healed we have to find a way to work together and support one another. When we experience interactions in which we feel "safe," we develop the ability to risk, to discuss, to work together, and to engage each other and finally, to build creatively!

Chapter 2

SITUATIONS

An African Tale: Nzambi had a daughter, which she sheltered until the day of her puberty until she was to go to the paint house and undergo purification. The daughter, at the time of her puberty, had to go to a distant village to undergo purification. At that time, Nzambi sent a slave to accompany her daughter. It was clear the daughter knew nothing of the world, when she asked about something the scrupulous slave would ask her for a piece of her clothing or adornments in exchange for the information. When Nzambi saw an animal, the slave would say, "Give me your clothes." After the exchange, the slave told her it was an antelope. This is the way it went until they came to the village. Ultimately, the slave appeared to be the princess and so was sent to the paint house while the princess was sent to toil in the fields as a slave. The princess would sing of her woe and the people, hearing her, though that she was mad. One day a trader walked by the young woman and she told him her story and asked where he was going. He said, "To the village of Nzambi." She related the story of her plight to the trader and asked that he inform the king and queen of the village of Nzambi. He did so. The King and Queen Nzambi came to the village and seeing her daughter in such a state ordered that the slave be burnt within the paint house. (Courlander, 1996).

This folktale from Zaire, demonstrates the agonizing plight of a neglected child when the facts remain hidden. Also, the child is ignored after trying to acknowledge his or her circumstances, usually because people want to live sensible lives where they are sure that this stuff does not happen because they never see it. Of course, neglect and worse things happen, but when pain is behind closed doors it is easy to ignore. Nzambi was a princess, I did not hold a high position like that, I did not have loving parents looking for me and desiring me to come home. I did have a person interested in my plight, though, not a trader but my grandmother.

In 1968, my hair was knotted into twists growing naturally that way from neglect since my hair had not been combed. I really paid very little attention to my hair. My sole interest was in getting food for my brother and myself. Like Nzambi, I knew very little about the world because as a neglected child I was locked away from it.

My mom would leave us and bolt the door from the outside. But we still managed to climb out a window in the bathroom. I was bony and agile then. I really did not think much about raking my knee across a nail or stepping on broken glass. I spent much of my time when I could get outside wondering around barefoot.

When we would escape to our grandmother's house, she would feed us and take us off to school. I did not mind school. I liked school because we got free lunches and sometimes that was the only hot meal that we got and I thank my grandma that we got that hot meal because she was the one that filled out the forms. I know that when I was at school, I did not think of my mother.

I never knew where my mother went when she locked us in. I will never know. I just know that we spent hours inside trying to find something to eat. One time we found potato flakes. I did not know anything about cooking but I remember how fluffy, hot mashed potatoes were. My brother and I found a pan and I got some matches and we decided to try and sneak and cook some mashed potatoes behind the sofa. I caught the couch on fire. We all were lucky that we did not burn alive because my mom locked the door from the outside with a pad lock so we could not get out by the door and the only other escape was the window.

I was beaten for that. I got beaten a lot. The worse was with the heel of my mom's high heel shoes. When I lay there bruised and bleeding, I felt nobody cared.

My brother and I would go to Hinkey's grocery store and take stuff to eat. I did not have any toys at this time, at least toys that my mother got us. I took these little tiny dolls. I guess I would take them because they were tiny and I could keep them hidden from my mom. I do not know if my brother took anything.

One time, my brother and I were in the store and we took food. The store manager caught us and he looked down on us. I think that is the first time that I realized that we were really something to pity. He looked at us and told is to keep what we had and warned us not to take anything else again. I could tell from his eyes though that he felt sorry for us. I knew than that I had no dignity.

We had no dignity, my brother and I. My brother and I were beaten severely for that transgression. The transgression of being hungry and taking food made us unworthy. My mom beat my brother with a wire clothes hanger over the head and shoulders. I remember because the hook stuck in his scalp and instead of pulling it out, my mother just yanked back and forth on it. It is amazing now how we rarely made a sound while she beat us. I wanted to escape.

I looked outside of the window and the sun shone brightly. I just wanted to be part of that light. I felt the warmth through my worn clothes and I just wanted to live there if God would permit it. During this period, we did not go to church. I do not know whether it was because my mom realized what condition we were in and did not want people to see us or she just did not care because of her schizophrenia. I will never know.

During this time, I mostly knew the four walls of that efficiency apartment. When we went to school, the kids, especially the girls begin teasing me about my hair. As I say like, Nzambi, I did not know much about anything. I thought at first it is my hair so what. But I begin to recognize that most of their hair was neatly pressed or plaited. And from what I knew no one had touched my hair for a long time and I had no mirror. This one girl, on the pretense of being nice (who knows maybe she was nice), offered to comb my hair. She came by with five of her friends and started raking that comb through my hair. She got it tangled, which did not take much, and pulled on the comb so hard that it brought tears to my eyes. She and her friends begin to laugh and tease me.

I begin to feel like an alien after that. Before my encounter with the girls, I knew that I did not have things. But I never bothered about not having things in the small world that my mother locked us into. For example, my brother and I would go out and play stick ball, if we were lucky we used a ball. If not, we hit rocks. We would escape out the window and play in the alley and then we would go back in before our mom got home. For some reason, she did not like it when we went to school either. I did not care. I ate a hot meal at school even though I did not come from the same world as the rest of the kids.

In my life, as with school, disparity existed. For example, at home, my mother was like the Tick Bird and my grandmother like lioness. A tick bird feeds off the parasites of animals such as hippos, as such they are useful creatures. My mother, due to her illness ran around in the streets, moved from place to place and lived off the scraps of others—her scattered focus turned her away us. Due mostly to neglect, we were taken away. Yet, my mom's presence in other people's lives seemed to lift them up while bringing her down. My grandmother, like the lion in many folktales, was loyal, strong and had the ability to see and sense things from a long way off.

By 1969, my mother had taken us back in forth from Illinois to Indiana to live in a string of poor or condemned housing. We returned to Illinois late that year and ended up living in this house with a red ball sticker on it. The red ball sticker indicated that the house was condemned to be torn down.

The house was very bug infested. One morning, I woke up and I had cockroaches crawling all over me. We had no food and my mom put a pad lock on the outside of the door and would pad lock us in. Sometimes, she would beat us.

During this time, my mom became pregnant with my second brother. She would eat in front of us and we would be so hungry. One time she had fried chicken. Afterward, I fished the bones from the garbage and cracked the bones with my teeth to get at the marrow. I got very sick after that. The next day, I woke up in a pool of blood with my mother beating on me and saying that I had picked my nose. I just lay there. I did not argue. I did not feel well and she just stopped hitting me because I think she was too tired to hit me anymore.

While we lived in this house, my mom tried to spray with insecticide. She used an over the counter spray and the roach infestation was so bad that the bugs streamed up the wall.

I can only remember one meal in that house. I mean just one meal, period. Mom boiled a pot of lentils. Unwashed lentils boiled to mush have the appearance of mud. My brother and I did not care. We ate them because we were very hungry.

When my mother was due to have my youngest brother, she sent me to get my grandmother. That is the only time I can remember when she ever sent me to my grandmother. My grandmother and uncle drove my mother to the hospital.

My mother had my youngest brother and brought him back to live in that condemned house. She would leave my two brothers and me in that house with no food. We did not know how to take care of my infant brother. I was eleven at that time and my other brother was seven. I did not know what to do. My infant brother would cry and cry.

I remember bouncing my tiny brother on the bed to get him to stop crying. Now as a middle-aged woman, I would have a fit if I saw somebody do what we did. But as an twelve-year-old left in charge of a newborn and eight-year-old with nothing to eat, little education, and locked in, I did not have many options.

My mom decided to have the house fumigated and locked us in with the baby in all those fumes. Someone reported it. The juvenile officers talked to us and asked us why we ran away. I showed them the half moon scars on my arms where my mother would dig her nails in me enough to draw blood.

They told us we would become wards of the state. This is when I was twelve. The older of my brothers was eight and my infant brother was six-days-old. That is when my grandmother went to court to petition for legal custody of us.

My grandmother was the lioness. In seeking to care for us, she did not want us to see our mother. A year after getting us, she sent my nine-year-old brother to live with our biological father. And she told me that I had to help with my youngest brother. I missed my brother and he is the only one who had shared experiences with me.

I know that my middle brother was so affected by my mom and how he lived that he had a hard time adjusting at our grandmother's house. He hoarded food. He continued to run away. He stood up to my grandmother. To her, he probably seemed difficult. To me, he was doing the things that we had always done to survive. With time, he might have been okay.

My heart broke more if that is possible. I missed my brother and I had to live in the house with my abusive uncle whom my grandmother doted on since he was "her baby." It was a miserable existence but it was still better than I had ever lived in my life since my parents separated eight years before. And I got to go to school everyday. School was an escape. But I lost my brother as an ally when my grandmother sent him away.

At least with my brother there were times we could trick my uncle. One time, my brother told my uncle that I was in the closet. We had a deep closet under the stairs. My uncle seeking any opportunity to corner me went in willingly. Then me and my brother both closed the door to the closet and locked it. We had to let him out when my grandmother got home but we spent most of the day in peace.

I put a lock on my bedroom door. The lock was an eye and hook type that you put on a screen door. Even with the lock, I got very little sleep. I became hyper vigilant. I also could not accept how blind my grandmother was to my uncle's behavior. For example, when I put the lock on my door he became very angry. He tried to convince her that I must be hiding something in my room. My grandmother, based on his accusations, did search my room only to find nothing. She took one look at where the latch and hook were and never bothered me again about it. [I visited the house later with my husband and showed him the door where the lock was and there were gouges in the door jam from my uncle trying to push his way in]. I revisited the house once I was on my true physical and spiritual journey of freedom, which brings me to another tale.

A West African Tale: A little shepherd boy, named Emeke, dreamed of flying. His grandmother told him to find the good snake and he would tell Emeke how to fly. Emeke shared his hope and dream of flying with the other villagers. They scoffed and laughed at him, especially the boys. Yet, Emeke held fast to his dream believing his grandmother's words. A strange occurrence happened one night. Near where he herded sheep, fireflies formed a circle in the air and in their light he saw animals heading toward a tree. He decided to follow reluctantly leaving his goats. In the tree, he saw a great snake. He asked the snake to help him fly believing it was the 'good snake' his grandmother spoke of. When Emeke asked the snake to fly the animals scoffed, especially the turtle. The turtle did not trust the snake. The snake directed Emeke as to what to do. The snake told Emeke to carry a rock, which would help him. Snake said he must build a kite in the shape of what is on the rock (the shape of a kite). Before the rains came, Emeke had to gather all the items to build the kite. Bark had to come from a baobab tree. Three large bamboo poles were needed to make the frame. Before "feast of harvest," Emeke must find the right wind to fly the kite. Before Emeke followed the snake's instructions, he returned to check on the goats. There hyena came and he said that he would watch them as he had asked the good snake for "patience and less greed." With the hyena herding the goats, Emeke tentatively left to gather the bark and bamboo. He came upon an elephant who had "wished to be kind and helpful" and showed Emeke where to find the baobab bark. Emeke went on and ran into a Rhino who already had the three cut pieces of bamboo waiting for him "who told him that he had made a wish "to be gentle and of service." With the help of the animals, Emeke was able to get everything before the rains came. But how could Emeke find the right wind? Emeke pondered the problem. On his return, his father, along with the village men were waiting. Before his father, Emeke was ashamed as his father discovered that Emeke did not do what he was told. Adding insult, he tried to explain that he allowed a hyena to guard the flock. The next day and days after Emeke was teased and teased, yet, he continued to build his kite to look like what was on the stone. He waited for the wind, fearing that it would not come and if it did, fearing that he would not recognize it. His grandmother continued to believe he would fly even when the rest of the family would not, even in the face of Emeke's own self-doubts. The right wind came, it whispered to him and he followed it to a great height. So great that he could see his village from high above and his reserve to fly grew weak. The wind encouraged him and he leapt. He soared and eventually floated back down to his family. All the villagers rejoiced. His grandmother was the first to embrace him and he danced with his grandmother while the drummer's sent thunder to the sky (Walter, 1985).

Although, I had an idea about the spheres of social influence that affected me as an adolescent, my understanding was rudimentary. My understanding was revealed primarily through my conformity, compliance, and obedience to rules and norms. My grandmother and school set the rules and norms that predominated in my life.

I did try to join into a peer group. I tried. First, I tried hanging out with kids from my old neighborhood. I found out very quickly that we did not have much to share in common anymore. I could talk about what had been and reminisce about the past. But what was important to me, was what was happening in my life now. I could not share what struggles I encountered in my classes, how the teachers were, what I was trying to learn. When I did, I was seen as a "geek." I even tried talking differently, using more "street talk" in order to be accepted but I found this to be very exhausting. In this way, I was left to try and socialize with the kids in my classes, the majority was Caucasian.

I tried hanging out with one of the girls from my class. I remember even going to that girl's house to stay the night. I remember feeling like an alien. I also soon discovered that no one came to my house. No one wanted to venture into my neighborhood. So, I relied and learned from the social spheres that provided me with the greatest cohesiveness and social support, my matriarchal family.

Looking back on my past and forward to my future, I see how the women on the maternal side of my family have influenced me. I still talk in different voices. I hear from my own mouth, the cherished voices of my maternal great-grandmother, my grandmother, my mother and myself. Using these voices sometimes gets me into trouble. I remember one time when I was volunteering in a home for troubled youth. We were making Easter Eggs. With the task complete, I asked one of the boys to put the eggs in "the ice-box." The child repeatedly said, "Are you sure?" A little annoyed, I became insistent using my grandmother's old phrase for the modern day refrigerator.

Later, we had to redo the two-dozen Easter Eggs. The child had placed the eggs in the freezer. All her life, my grandmother referred to the refrigerator as the icebox. I guess that I picked up the habit. Although it made for a good laugh for all involved, using the words "ice-box" was a lesson to me of how easy our valued caretakers can become our voices.

I am strong and all the women in my family indicated that they were strong too. My great-grandmother, an African American woman with a light, skin tone, grew up around the turn of the century. She was orphaned and passed from family to family. It seems no one wanted a "light-skinned colored girl with shock red hair." She grew up to successfully raise five children, four girls and one boy. She had to do this single-handed as her husband left early on. She was hard and bitter and she made sure it showed. She had a double-barrel shotgun that she kept for intruders. She filled it with buckshot. She also made her own beer. Even as a child, I learned that she was "rough on rats" tough. My great grandmother's house was near the projects. Or rather they built projects near my great grandmother's house. For anyone not familiar with a project, it was a collection of multi-family dwellings designed to provide housing for the poor. Typically, they became over crowded and run down. My great-grandmother had family who wanted her to live with them but she was determined to live and die in her own home and aside from a tornado nothing was going to move her. She passed that tenacity on to us.

Once, my grandmother had some pressing business she wanted to share with my great grandmother. We grandchildren had been visiting at the time. In my great grandmother's generation, children were seen and not heard. So, she sent my brother Jimmy and I to go play on the project's playground. A group of kids came out and bullied us off threatening to "beat us up if we came back to their place." So we quickly returned to my great grandmother's house. My great grandmother greeted us at the door and asked why we had returned. I explained and she said if we did not go and face those kids and play at the park which was for everyone she was going to give us a "switching." I feared as well as revered my great grandmother and we returned. The kids came back and I told them I would rather take a beating from them then my great grandmother and to my surprise they left us alone. But all the joy was gone out of wanting to play and I can remember just idly sitting in the swing wishing to go back to my grandmother's. My great grandmother showed gentleness and love through her actions.

Without spoken words, she let us know we were loved. We would go over and have homemade peanut brittle. She would cook the peanut brittle and pour it out to cool on some waxed paper spread on her kitchen counter top. Grand-momma White, what we called her because of her white hair, would leave the peanut brittle that way and let us break it. When I was a teenager, she offered to teach me to crochet. I thought I knew it all and did not appreciate that people do not last forever. Now looking back, I wish that I had her teaching me to crochet. I imagine that through her teaching me, I would have learned so much more about her life and struggles. The biggest lesson that I learned from my great-grandmother is that other people's expectations are not more important than yourself and your own needs. Self-hate leads to self-abasement, which gets in the way of loving others (Backus & Chapian, 1985). My great grandmother had learned to love herself even with the odds stacked against her and she passed that love onto others.

My great-grandmother provided love to others on her terms. Because she was so different looking among her peers, she did not get a lot of respect. As a consequence, my great-grandmother learned from an early age that everyone else's approval was not essential to her peace of mind. She also became self-reliant as a consequence. And I adapted that attitude from her. And thankfully, she had my grandmother, whom she loved and relied on. My grandmother, who is the oldest of the five, quit high school to help take care of her sisters and brother.

My grandmother's hands shaped me. Becoming mine and my brother's legal guardian when I was twelve, she caught me at an age where I was ready to please. I wanted so much to be liked and appreciated. I see now that her actions more than her words taught me lessons of devotion, perseverance and determination. I cannot say that my younger brothers learned the lessons in the same way. For twenty three years, I have had no contact with Jimmy who would now be 43-years-old. My last memory of Jimmy before was when he was a child around nine-years-old when he left to live with our biological father. My other half-brother, shares with his father's talent for music and a love of alcohol. At age 35, he has turned his life around and my hope is that he may, one day, write a book as well.

For me, my grandmother was my salvation. My best memory of my grandmother is gardening with her. With her back against the sun, she appeared substantial, like a granite stature, everlasting. I was not into hugging as so much had happened to me. I almost could not stand to be touched. So, I would stand close to her and she smelled like the earth. And like the earth, she was nurturing, warm and encouraged growth. And also like the earth, if you showed disrespect she could turn you upside down and inside out before you had a handle on what just happened. The biggest lesson that I learned from my grandmother was that loving others is not a set of obligations. She took us in freely and chose to love us at a time when she could have retired. She was hard and old-fashioned, although she was open to listening her word was final. Unfortunately,

I begin to enter adolescence with hormones raging at the same time society was changing.

In 1971, things were changing. Respect to authority, which once seemed so important was being questioned and challenged. People appeared to be more selfish. Perhaps, because I started to enter puberty after my grandmother got guardianship of my brothers and me, I started to see the world differently. Everything was changing. The corner one-penny store went away, the downtown went away. The mall came. People who hung out on the street now you would not want to talk to. "I remember when," a phrase I swore that I would never use, began to enter my vocabulary.

The place that I grew up in, the "North-end" of Champaign, Illinois, was no longer the place I have come to know. People began to die for "unnecessary" reasons. For example, a twelve-year-old boy shot a man in his car because it was part of the boy's gang initiation. A man was stabbed to death because the other man was angry. Another man was stabbed in a back alley because "who knows why?" Violence was an everyday occurrence and becoming part of the social fabric of my neighborhood. This was the era I grew up in and it was difficult.

This growing up period was the hardest because I had only my grandmother's voice to spur me on with my education. Like Emeke, I was taunted and teased at my old school. Because my grandmother wished to help my uncle purchase a new house in Urbana, we moved in with them to help with the house payments. I had to switch from a Champaign school to a school in Urbana, Illinois. For one semester, we lived with my uncle and the new kids teased me too. My abusive uncle came along with us and probably because he was feeling stress began to take his frustration out on me. At school, I fell on some marble steps. My knee looked like a grapefruit. When it was just beginning to heal, my uncle re-injured my knee by throwing something at it without any warning. All I could do was go to my bedroom, lie down on my bed, and cry. During this time, my grandmother was successful in helping my other uncle and his new wife to purchase a home and we lived with them in Urbana until they became financially stable.

I could remember wanting so much to please everyone. I did not want to be turned out. I fell on marble steps at the school. For years, my knee would slip out of joint yet as great as the pain was, I dare not complain. In my 40s, I had surgery to repair problem. My other uncle, whom I came to refer to in my mind as 'the mean one' re-injured my knee by throwing a hair-pick at it. You might laugh to think a hair pick? Come on? But back than a hair pick, at least the one he had was a large item with wide teeth and made of a metal alloy and it had an eight-inch handle. When the pick hit my knee it hurt badly. He knew I did not dare tell my grandmother because I did not want to make waves. I am still not very confrontational but I no longer look at pleasing everyone like I did when I was an adolescent. Back then I was still very fragile and would allow the demands of others to lead to expectations of myself that left me feeling hurt, unloved, rejected, unwanted, unworthy, and angry. I kept searching for an identity and the move did not help.

The move to Urbana then back to Champaign, its twin city, made me undergo an educational adjustment. Champaign's Edison Junior High School did not have the class equivalents that Urbana had. My choice was to go into advanced classes or technical classes. My grandmother signed me into advance classes. Thus, entering Junior High School (grades 7 through 9) was a life course event. Most of the students in my classes were Caucasian. Save for Ramona, why after all these years do I remember her name. I do because she was the only other African American female in all my math classes Geometry, Trigonometry and Analytical Geometry. Most of the students in all my classes were Caucasian. I liked school but I had to work very hard. People tried to sabotage me along the way. My Trigonometry Teacher knew his topic well but seemed only to explain it to those who already understood it. I did not know the material well and I needed more assistance. That assistance was never to come.

In class, he never offered assistance and one time when I insisted on getting help from him he said in a loud, demeaning voice: "You should know this by now!" My Trigonometry teacher would also make humiliating comments about the way I walked, talked, and laughed any time he saw me outside of the class. I talked to my grandmother and we went to the principal together to ask that I be transferred to another class. The principle said that he could not do that since it was mid-semester and that he would take our concerns under consideration. After that meeting, the teacher stepped up his campaign of innuendos inside and outside of the classroom. I never gave up though and each day my grandmother, although she could not help me with the mathematics would say, "I know that you are trying." I stuck to it and got through but I knew my next class was Analytical Geometry and I had to know Trigonometry. Thankfully, Mrs. Hill (funny how I forgot the Trigonometry teacher's name) was a fantastic teacher. Not only was she knowledgeable; she also sincerely wanted students to learn. She remembered my situation because I had wanted to transfer to her class. Understanding my concerns, she set me up with a high school tutor for trigonometry. I literally had to learn trigonometry while I was doing my Analytical Geometry class. As a young person growing up studying like this most of my life, I felt resentful. I felt, "how dare that guy treat me that way and get away with it." He could and did—he was the teacher. Periodically, although I did my utmost to avoid him, I would run into him in the hall. I would hear my grandmother's voice at these times especially. Her belief in education was strong. "Education was something no one can take away," she would say. At those times, I would close my ears, press my chin to my chest as I squeezed my books and walk on by that teacher. A heavy workload was a blessing because I did not have room in my mind for the reverberations of the internalized taunts of my uncle or time to think about the lonely life that I was leading.

But also like Emeke, I gained valuable knowledge by the encounters that I had with different people, in Emeke's case it was animals. However, like Emeke, I found individuals along the way who were willing to sacrifice of their time and talents. I also had a grandmother who believed in me and was willing to allow me to make my own choices, and to even to fail. Even though she had a low tolerance level for bad behavior, she allowed me to make decisions affecting our household. I learned, like Emeke to be self-confident, motivated, and ready for the real world because I learned responsibility in helping to care for my youngest brother, dealing with schoolwork on my own, paying some bills, and working summers.

Cline and Fay (1990) wrote:

> "Responsible kids, Irresponsible kids. The most responsible kids I (Jim) encountered in my three decades in education were the kids at an inner city school where I served as an assistant principal. They all hailed from federally funded housing projects. Those kids woke up in the morning without an alarm clock and got to school in time for breakfast without any assistance from their parents.

They knew that if they got there, they got breakfast; if they didn't, they missed it. They never missed a bus when it was going someplace they wanted to go.

The most irresponsible kids I ever saw were in upper-middle-class suburban school. The first day of school a thousand kids arrived in eighteen different buses. Half of these kids ran straight to the playground for some pre-bell frolic. The other half raced directly to the principal's office to phone their folks for forgotten registration materials, coats, and lunches.

Responsible behavior has a direct correlation to the number of decisions children are forced to make. The more they make decisions; the more responsible they become (p. 48).

I had to make a lot of decisions on my own. I won't say it was easy. There were times that I gave up activities that many of my peers enjoyed, such as dances, youth programs, concerts, and after school programs to care for my brother, prepare dinner for the family, or clean, or cut the grass, or whatever to help my family keep going. Some times, I felt resentful but I also felt needed at home.

What dampened the resentment and the feelings of being slighted was my grandmother's sincere and loving concern. For the most part, my life had only natural consequences, as my grandmother recognized that I was older. So, I was able to connect any misbehavior that I had to the consequences and not blame my grandmother. Because of her empathy and grief when I did something wrong, I tried my best to do my best. I did not want to disappoint her. As a consequence, I came more loving, skillful, and capable and like Emeke was able to fly above my circumstances. Also like Emeke, I love my village and my family-of-origin; I just had to follow my dream.

Chapter 3

BELONGINGNESS

An African Tale: Once there was a girl with beautiful, large eyes. The men of her village were captivated whenever she would pass by and glance at them. One of the girl's chores was to fetch water for her family. This was not a simple task because the village and surrounding area were suffering from a drought. The girl would have to walk a long while. On one particular day, she was walking along a riverbed whose muddy bottom yielded no signs of fresh water when a fish of many colors popped up from the mud. The beautiful fish made a promise to the girl to fetch the clearest water for her. Thus, each day the girl went and talked to the fish and the fish fetched clear water for her. The two fell in love. On the seventh day, she embraced the fish and they became husband and wife. Her family, although pleased to get the clean, cold water everyday, were curious about where it came from. Her father a witchdoctor was determined to find out where it came from and feared that his daughter had a spell on her. He turned his son into a fly and as a fly he hid in the water jug. On the girl's meeting and talking with the fish, the brother flew off to their father and reported what he saw. The men of the family returned to the spot and killed the fish fearing that the discovery of the fish married to her would be disgraceful and shameful to the family. When the girl returned they led her dead husband at her feet. She knew in her mind that if they killed her husband they may also kill the child she carried, so she returned to the river to drown herself. As she waded into the water her many children were born and took the form of water lilies. (Lester, 1992)

Maybe this story stood as a warning not to marry anyone so different from your self. A warning with the message: Stay within the village because to venture outside of it meant disgrace and death to all. Or as I prefer to see it, it is a story of love or love's essence that is unstoppable even unto death as indicated by the water lilies. The story also conveys to me the sacrifice of love, through the fish, by ending up losing his life to risk seeing the girl. I also consider the great loss to her family who will now have to go back to drinking muddy water because they could not see beyond the fish's difference to the gift that he had provided them.

Blind love of another in a world that is inhospitable to difference is like "trying to breath under the burdens of the world" (Bell, 1992, p. 34). Yet, like the girl with large eyes I fell in love with a man who has a different skin color from my own. Because of this pigmentation disorder [according to the rest of the world], we have had our share of difficulties. The biggest issue that people outside of relationship failed to understand is that we did not get together because we were lonely, needy, attracted by difference, or wanting something exciting and difference. We got together because we loved one another. We loved each other with no strings attached. We did not have conditional love. Before he became my husband, Mark helped my family and me with no obligation. I, thankfully, recognized his genuine love and married the man. But it took me time to get to that point. I had encountered many pitfalls before I accepted Mark's marriage proposal.

Prior to attending the University of Illinois where I met my husband, I attended Parkland Junior College. While at Parkland, I met my first boyfriend. We dated often. However, our relationship ended in disaster. We came from two different religious backgrounds, he was Bahai and I had been going back to Methodist church with a co-worker. I was invited by a friend who was Bahai to a potluck and that is how I met Jim. I liked Jim's quiet ways and he seemed so knowledgeable. He was going to graduate from the University of Illinois in Meteorology. I thought a lot of him.

I know, at the time, being a weather man was kind of a boring thing. This is before they had Cable's Weather Channel. But I was impressed by what he knew and he showed me where they read maps and measurements to find out what is going on in order to make forecasts and predictions.

I hate to admit that at this late date, I just was beginning to develop interdependent relationships with friends and relatives that were more healthy and appropriate. I visited my grandmother and helped out when she needed. I took my baby brother to the movies, the park, or just walking.

I felt guilty about leaving both my grandmother and brother under the tyranny of my uncle who still expected my grandmother to wash his clothes and cook his meals. I began making friendships with people at school and at work. I enjoyed their company and did not have to worry so much about how I looked to others. I felt I was beginning to stand on more solid ground with my relationships with others.

Then the day came when my boyfriend decided to head to Washington, DC. He felt that his prospects were better there. Being young and impressionable, I wanted nothing more than to go with him. He looked at me directly and said that I really did not care about him very much and I would found out how much I didn't when I got a little older. He said that all I wanted to do was get away from my uncle and that is not a good reason to commit to a relationship. He moved away and I was heartbroken.

I decided to go visit him in Washington. I called and he said that it was okay and that he had missed me too. I came to see him and stayed at a hotel. I spent a great deal of my savings to come and see him and I was not sure what I was going to do next. I just wanted to see him. But it was no longer me he was interested in, it was sex. And although, I caved into what he wanted, I just felt dead inside.

I left and went back to college. I slipped into a deep depression and lost two weeks of school. One of my computer professors was understanding and talked with me honestly about just finishing with a certificate. He recognized that I did not have the stamina at that point and recommended that I continue with my psychology courses. I did not want to admit it but just getting to school had become a chore. I did keep going though I felt distraught and could not seem to fully concentrate. This was the worse time possible for me to enter into another relationship. But following my human nature, instead of the wisdom that resided in my head I went and got involved in a new relationship.

On the rebound, during this time when I was still pretty vulnerable, I met another guy. I would know Bob for three awful years. He was physically abusive. By all outward appearances, except to his parents which he also, I suspect abused (I saw him kick his dad), we were a couple.

In the year that I met Bob, I did have fun and interesting experiences. My counselor, at the time, recommended that I try the college's theatre and I got to know people. I learned the lines to plays. Although the people that I met were kind of quirky, they just did not approach life the same way as everyone else.

Bob was taking set design and doing lighting for the play, The Miracle Worker, in which I got a small role in. I had fun memorizing the lines and learning about the history behind the play. Despite all odds, the heroine, Helen Keller learned how to communicate with others. Despite being deaf and blind, Ms. Keller went on to write her autobiography. I felt encouraged by her story. But the reality of my life struck what little encouragement that I had gained out of me.

Bob became increasingly abusive. All the mental tapes that I had learned earlier has a child from my uncle, begin to play over and over again. I found words even surfacing to my own mouth defacing my own self. How stupid I was? What a dummy? Moron? What was I thinking about? If it was not for making mistakes, I wouldn't be doing anything. I had someone in my corner to help me but I was not ready to listen.

My counselor tried to get me to see that this relationship was not working. She just would ask me to consider things like how he talked to me. I wanted to remain in denial. Instead of reexamining my relationship with Bob, I broke off my counseling support. I can see now why Bob and I were attracted to each other. He lacked self-esteem and was looking for someone to build him up. I was still being a walking victim. I did not, at the time, want to examine my choices. I let my life be consequence of the circumstances that I find myself in rather than choosing a direction for myself.

At the age of 19, I managed to get a room on the University of Illinois campus. I felt lonely but was happy to have gotten away from my Uncle. What I did not realize is that I had traded my uncle's type of domination for another type.

By the time I transferred to the University of Illinois, at the age of 19, I was already beat down. I kept taking Bob back though. One time, he took my head and slammed it into a dumpster. Thankfully, the gash was where my eyebrow was and he did not crack my skull. The person that worked on my face was a surgeon and he stitched the gash up within my eyebrow so that the hair grew back over it but if I run my fingers over the spot, I can still feel it.

I ended up in the hospital twice and the police came and interviewed me. They interviewed me with Bob standing right there. The last time he beat me up; he came through my bedroom at night at the boarding house where I rented a room. He must have shinnied up to the window somehow. I do not remember him beating me. What I do remember is waking up with my hand gashed open and my bed was full of pee. He had beaten me up, I later found out, and then peed on me. As a consequence of this fight and the commotion and damage it caused, I had to move.

So, I had no place to stay and I had to ask my grandmother if I could come back and live with her. I offered to pay her so much a month when I found work. Yes, I had lost my job too.

Even with all that, I still continued to see Bob. I was not ready to stop being his punching bag. His temper was violent and quick and came often without warning or provocation. We were walking along one day, just down the street and he decided to kick me in my legs with his steel reinforced work boots. I do not know how I continued to stand but I knew that if I had fallen to the ground; he would have continued to kick me maybe in my stomach or head.

Towards the end of this sour relationship, I got a full-time job working at a medical information lab. I did computer operation and data entry. I got an efficiency apartment. Bob asked me how come I could get a job and he could not. For the first time, I really started seeing him as what he was to my life—a roadblock. I did everything in my power to avoid him. I tried breaking up with him and he just would not hear it.

One time I came home and found him sitting in my apartment. He must have come through a window. He punched me in the stomach so hard that I fell to the floor then he left. When I got my wind back I called my grandmother, she helped me gather up his clothes and we scattered them on the lawn as we laughed with glee.

I know that it was really his grandmother's house and he and his parents lived there but I did not care. I felt like I was being set free.

That night, my grandmother let me stay at her house.

He stopped coming around the apartment although I had to call the police to convince him that I was serious. But he did not stop hanging around where I worked. He shadowed me everywhere that I went until I got jumpy and thought that I saw him all the time.

It got so bad that my supervisor called me into a meeting and said that if I did not do something about Bob, I could lose my job. I knew better than confront Bob, especially alone. So, I told the supervisor that the next time that I saw him around work that I could call the police. That seemed to get the supervisor off of my back. However, I knew in my heart that the police could not or would not do anything unless he assaulted me again. This is before the domestic violence and stalking laws that they have now. I knew from experience that I did not have too many options.

Around this time, I met the man who was going to be my husband. Mark is brave enough to go into a Women's Lingerie department and buy me a sensible brassier without blushing. But it was not always like this. I was too blind to behold this gem in my life and looking back it appears that God was putting him in my way.

I kept praying about how lonely I was. How, I would never take anything from anybody again and I kept running into my husband. I was so blind that I went out with his housemate, not knowing they were housemates, and ran into him in the hall while I was waiting for his housemate to change. I really did not want to get seriously involved with anybody. I think that I was more or less looking for a drinking buddy. I do not know what happened to his housemate. I know that we dated once and I saw Mark ever since.

When Mark and I decided to date, I felt that I went from one fragile moment to another. We went to a parade on the hottest day of the year and this man lugged a cooler all the way there and back in ninety degree weather under the burning sun and with heavy humidity. I decided to cook him pizza with my new pizza maker and made the crust so hard it was like concrete. He sat there, smiling through the meal, and said it was good. I gave up trying to eat it, cooked some pasta, and scraped the top off of the pizza onto the pasta. Yes, the pizza was that bad. But Mark endured the pizza, as with other challenges to come, willingly and without fuss. Mark even faced the matter of my own lack of self-acceptance.

I felt low about myself but he did not seem to see it. I made the same disparaging remarks that I had when I was with Bob. But Mark seemed to ignore that altogether. He would tell me that he saw me helping my grandmother, going to work, and trying to go to school. He saw me helping my brother. I begin to see myself through his eyes and somewhere along the line I stopped beating my own self up verbally. My head sometimes reverberated with those awful, insidious thoughts about my personal inadequacy as a human. And Bob, still remained as a proverbial thorn in my side with his emotional abuse.

Bob still continued to harass me. He would come around my apartment building yelling my name. Even though I moved, he found out where I lived. He must have followed me from work, which would not have been hard as I either walked or rode my bike. Once, he banged on my door so hard he put a hole in it. I did not feel secure anywhere. I felt that I had to always watch over my shoulder. Although both Mark and I were wary of this situation with Bob, we decided that nothing would stand in the way of our being together.

Mark and I decided to move in together to save expenses. It was an uneasy relationship. I admit that I drink too much and I stressed over everything. At the age of 22, I developed an ulcer and was prescribed ulcer medications. In this year, 1981, more things started to happen to me, I had to have a cystocopy and in office urethral dilation. These are minor operations, but I personally thought very painful. But through these trials, Mark and I persevered.

After living together for three years, Mark and I decided to get married. In 1985, in front of a justice of the peace, a very blustery and rainy day we said our vows to each other. We had a three-day honeymoon. At this point, my youngest brother, who came to live with us on a permanent basis, had been with us for two and half years. My brother had to come live with us because our grandmother became very ill.

I had to call my uncles to come and get her. Her house was a wreck. Her boarders let the dog run wild in the house and dog feces everywhere. There was food and garbage everywhere. The house was in terrible condition. But my new husband and I cleaned it up and when we were done we had filled sixteen large garbage bags, the kind you use for leaf pickup, with garbage of everything imaginable. We started our cleanup with shovels. I had to swallow my gall more than a few times.

We did get the house cleaned up and my uncle sold it. He never even talked to us again. He never offered us any compensation not that I was expecting any. But I did think that he would leave me one thing from my grandmother. I wanted some keepsake; however, small.

The other issue was caring for my brother who became really unruly after that. He kept running away. He said he blamed me for our grandmother being taken away. He resented my taking care of him since I was only his sister.

With a new husband, all the personal and family of origin situations were hard, after which, I found out that I was pregnant. I was happy about it but then I got laid off from work. I managed to buy myself a computer and I walked part-time at the YMCA and between the two jobs and my husband's fellowship, we managed to survive. Then, I had a miscarriage. I did not have enough money to pay for a procedure to remove the dead baby because I did not completely miscarry. I refused to believe the baby was dead and went on bed rest but I was just making myself sick physically and eventually had to go in for what they called a d and c (A dilatation and curettage) for a missed abortion (abortion is the medical word for miscarriage). I had it done in the office and we kept the rest of the money his mom sent us to help out with living expenses. My legs shook terribly and I cried uncontrollably. My pain did not end there.

For days after, I felt as if someone drew a black veil over my head and I could no longer see or think clearly. I just worked. I became hard hearted. I remember asking my brother for a glass of water when I was miscarrying, afraid to move, trying to hold on to that baby with my will. My brother refused. He told me years later that he thought I carried a grudge because of that. I admit that I was very angry but his overall behavior gave me call for concern. I still remember the details of that day and wish that I could wish it away. I never got adequate counseling for that period of my life. I had been four months pregnant just when you can begin to feel faint movements. Thinking about it, still brings me to tears. But I refuse to re-victimize myself by simply ruminating over the circumstances.

Somehow, I know it was God, I pulled out of the "blues" I went into. We eventually ran out of money and the YMCA fired me. They had hired me into a new position because one of their workers left but then she decided to come back and they wanted to put me back folding towels when I said that I wanted to keep my job they fired me. I hope that place since is supposed to be Christian recognizes what the supervisor did.

We ended up coming to the Upper Peninsula of Michigan to live with my husband's mom. Out of money and with no idea of what our prospects would be. However, my brother was college ready and would be entering in the fall. We had survived three years of marriage.

Chapter 4

AFFINITY

An East African Tale: A woman and her beautiful daughter, Nsangi, lived in a cave near a village. In those days, gorillas could talk and would often trick people and eat them. To protect themselves, the women and the girl rolled a big stone in front of the entranceway to the cave. The woman had to leaver everyday to trade in the village. She would leave her daughter in the cave. Upon returning to the cave, the woman sang the girl a special song so the girl would know that it was her mother, which approached. One day, a gorilla watched the mother singing to her daughter. The gorilla practiced the song with a plan to trick the girl into thinking it was the mother and remove the stone so it could eat her. On the first day, the gorilla sounded terrible and the girl did not remove the stone. Overtime though, the gorilla practiced and practiced. Soon there came a day when the gorilla sounded just like her mother, the girl removed the stone and before she could react to her mistake she was swallowed up whole. The mother came home and lamented to see her daughter gone. She returned to the village to seek help and was told to take heart. If they could find the gorilla that ate her daughter, the girl was still alive and whole in one of its fingers. One by one, the woman had to confront each gorilla asking about her daughter. One by one they denied everything. When they came to the last gorilla, he sings very badly and looked so guilty when he denied everything they knew it had to be him. His finger was slit and the girl spring forth. He than was chased far away from the village (Serwadda, 1987).

Attitudes influence relationships with others, individual and group behavior, and self-awareness. Since attitudes shape our social cognition and influence our social behavior, their influence can be seen in different aspects of our life, such as work, interpersonal relationships, health, etc. There are two issues that strongly impact our attitudes and affinity to one another.

Two of the biggest issues that underlie the surface tension of our everyday lives are racism and discrimination. One of the most important things all of us need to do is to tell ourselves and others the truth in order to change our behaviors and cognitions (Backus & Chapian, 1985; Rutstein, 1993). What often happens is that if we are victims of racism and discrimination, we often try to mask our hurt and persevere. Worse, we may identify with our persecutors, internalize the oppression. Internalized oppression is when oppressed people internalize many of the stereotypes that people have of their group and apply it to their own people (Brown & Mazza, 1998). A stereotype is a prejudicial attitude often based on a simple generalization about a particular group. As painful as it is to state some of these prejudicial attitudes, some examples are: all African Americans are poor, all women are needy and emotional, and all Japanese are rich and out for money. The point is that hearing these over and over can make the victim begin to believe and adopt these attitudes toward members of his or her own group. The internalization of prejudicial attitudes occur based on stereotypes about gender, race, ethnicity, culture, etc. It is worse when the truth is hidden among families interferes with the ability of the family to handle real crises.

My uncle did not take me seriously when I asked him to come get his mother. To him, I was being a hysterical woman. I imagine to him, after having a sister like my mom, he thought that I was just going through routine womanly histrionics. I had to fight to represent myself in a way so that I could convince him that I was helping his mother the best that I could. However, I felt it was his turn to help care for his mother. She needed more help than I had the resources for. I remember talking to my uncle and explaining how frustrated I was.

In helping my grandmother in her advancing years, I begin to rage against the sky. When she became seriously sick due to chronic diabetes and high blood pressure, she kept getting hospitalized because of poor diet. I called one of my uncles, her son, for help. He laughed. I said I am serious. At the time I was working full-time and going to school part-time and caring for my younger brother. It was all too much for him, the only mom he ever knew (my grandmother took us on when he was only six-years-old), was going to be separated from him. Perhaps, it was too much for me too. I did not think about what I was taking on at the age of twenty-two, I just knew that I was the oldest, I was there and it was expected. I also had the same issues with health care providers regarding my not being taken seriously. And some were indeed Gorillas, pretending to be helpful, using my language, and at the same time telling me that you can't sign this form or you can't do that.

Whether it was due to ageism, as I did look and act young, sexism, or racism or some combination it was a challenge to get my grandmother health care assistance. I am sure that my grandmother's noncompliance with her medical plan of care did not help. I did sincerely want to gain help for her and it was an exhausting process. But it was no more exhausting a process than what my grandmother went through to help my brothers and me.

My grandmother saved me from ruin and I wanted to help her anyway that I could. Thirty-years later, I still cannot talk about the possible ruin that I faced but the truth of it must reside in my eyes. Sometimes, not as often these days, my husband asks what is troubling me and I just cannot say. I tried to help my grandmother and my uncles did come to retrieve her. Her house was a mess. She had taken boarders in who had turned out to be petty criminals and destroyed the house looking for papers. Truthfully my husband and I went in with shovels and scooped up sixteen garbage bags full of debris, food, trash and animal feces before we could get down to the real cleaning. This happened over a matter of months during a period that my grandmother refused to see me and now I know why. My uncle did come to retrieve her eventually. I felt relief at her being taken care of by her son.

But my relief was short-lived. My uncle, the one I trusted, had turned out to be a Gorilla too. He had placed her in the care of the abusive uncle. But maybe he was being sincere, like the villager and thought she was closer to Gregory. Or an even simpler explanation is that he did not want to be bothered. Whatever the reasons, the outcome was the same, a bad living situation for her.

She had been there for only two months when she was hit by an automobile. We had just moved in with my husband's mother because we too began to face financial difficulties after I was laid-off from one position and fired from another (yes I had taken on a second job). My husband's fellowship ran out as well and we still had my brother to get off to college. My grandmother did not die instantly and lingered for almost two weeks, losing one leg with the possibility of losing the other.

I wanted to make sense of what had happened in my mind. I called my uncle, the eldest of my grandmother's two sons, and he informed me that my grandmother had never stayed with him. She moved in with the younger uncle and they had had an argument. I could picture my grandmother having an argument with my uncle, stepping out of the house to go walking and not paying attention to where she was. I could see her in my mind's eye stepping of f of the curb. A few days before our move to Marquette from Champaign, my grandmother had called me and asked that I come and get her. I failed to do for her what she had done for me eleven years before when my grandmother had taken us to.

Even knowing that I was a newly wed, a guardian to my brother and in financial trouble was not enough to settle my heart about my decision not to help my grandmother at that time I hope that she can forgive me in heaven. As the girl in the story, I had rolled the stone away in the hope of meeting "mother," which to me is symbolic of my own desire for spiritual provender. I needed sustenance in the form of social support in this lean time and my need remained unmet. My uncle was a gorilla. He said what I wanted to here and I let my grandmother go.

When she died my world shifted. I truly became part of my husband's family. When my brother left for college, his absence also reopened the heartache of my past experiences. I really felt a blank hole after my youngest brother had lived with my husband and me for six years. It was also a feeling of relief to know that his feet were set on his own life path because it was hard living under my mother-in-law's roof. My life had taken a 180-degree turn. I was going back to college and working in the cafeteria in the pot wash area as I had done when I went to the University of Illinois back when I was nineteen-years-old. I did not see a way out then.

Even though, God never gave up on me, I begin relying on my anger. I stayed in my room most of the day. Venturing out only to look for jobs, I finally found one doing data-entry for a local paper and shortly after, a matter of three weeks, I became ill with a bad case of flu. What I did not know then was that I also had asthma. I had a high fever but I kept on working. I remember having difficulty holding my head up. The nausea was terrible but I kept going. One day, I just could not get up. I had not been eaten and I just could not get up. I called work and they told me that I had to come in. I said that I could not risk losing my job but I could not get up. They told me if I could not come in now then don't bother coming in ever.

My mother-in-law came downstairs telling me that the business had called to ask if I was sick and she came to check on me. She touched my forehead and said alarmed, "You really are sick!" She made me some turkey soup. I broke down at that point and told her that I did not think that I could bear my grandmother's dying.

My mother-in-law introduced me to her Catholic Church. I was raised Baptist, yet I was familiar with orthodox Catholicism through my cousins. She agreed to be my sponsor for two-years through the RCIA program. I attended church in the mornings usually after working as a Certified Nurse's Aid nights. I also attended college part-time. I had to switch from the food service job to CNA because it paid better and I enjoyed working with older people. At one point school became a nightmare because of a poor internship placement. But do to a good field instructor, a good friend and a new, successful internship placement I survived. Also, in attending church, I had a chance to quiet my mind and to give my troubles over to God.

At a time when I wanted to scream at the world and yell at the sky, I was able to have this quiet peace at church. I truly felt physical calm. I still felt along alone though. I used to solely blame this rather parochial community. I did not recognize that my due to unresolved anger I became distrustful, cautious. I did not have an open heart required for personal growth. Also because of this, I had a diminished capacity to discern who meant well and who did not. A friend of mine recommended that I pray for discernment. Deep down, I knew I would be okay at school. I wrote in my journal in 1995, "I also have questionable intellect; but, like a professor told me once I am resourceful. I am also diligent, what I like for in brains I make up for in persistence.

She told me to rest. I eventually got better, more from her caring and soup, than anything. I lost that job. But as they say when one door closes; another opens. I got a job as a unit clerk at the hospital in the Emergency Room. I think that I lasted there about six weeks before deciding to go back to college to double major in psychology and social work. My turning point at the job was that the position was based on a clinical ladder as with nursing and you were required to do so many duties with each month. I remember an experienced clerk directing me to do something and than writing the duty on her paper. I questioned it as I had actually done the work. She said because she had showed me that she could take credit performing the duty. I said at this rate I would not get anything on my sheet. As the first months, would include direction from others. During my health screening, a doctor patted me on the head. I found work in school to be rewarding but I still had to work and pay my bills. My life went full-circle because I got a job as a student-assistance in the food service at the local university, which was similar to my job when I first left home at

18-years-old. I paid for my schooling out of pocket and when I graduated from Northern Michigan University, I did not owe anything.

Education, as my grandmother had identified early on, seemed to be where I shined. I went on to Wayne State University's Advanced Standing Social Work Program. I make that sound so easy don't I? Actually, I did not think I had a chance to get into graduate school. God's mercy is wide and deep as the ocean though and I filled out three applications: one to Wayne, one to University of Chicago and one to Michigan State University. I could only send off three applications because I could only afford entrance fees for three colleges and I only wanted advanced standing programs in the Midwest. I figured that if I did not get into graduate school then I would work. There was always something out there for me. I did get the letter and the choices I made from then on centered on my decision to go to graduate school. My last semester of undergraduate school was the hardest because I knew I would leave. I would have to leave, my family, my two little boys for a year. My mother-in-law questioned. "How could I leave my family?" My husband seemed less supportive the usual. The boys were sad. But somehow, I held together.

My mother-in-law helped me get settled in my efficiency on campus. She drove me down to Wayne. My brother-in-law lived and Dearborn and we stayed there the night before my program's entry colloquium, registration only traveler's checks and a little cash, she wrote out a check for my deposit. I agreed to her financial help and to pay her back, and did, pay back to her over time. I was overwhelmed by her willingness and generosity to help me.

As well as I did. I did not have an attitude of humility. I was angry. I wanted to battle the world. Now, looking back, I had not gotten over feeling that I had abandoned my grandmother. I begin to think negatively about things. I became yoked to mistrust. I left the Upper Peninsula of Michigan to go to Detroit to attend Wayne State University with a seared conscious; nothing could get close to heal my spirit. Thankfully, there was free counseling service on campus. I was able to work through some of things that I could not do by myself. So, I was feeding my mind and soothing my emotions but I still was not developing my spirit. I was beginning to know other people. I was "breaking out of my nut of loneliness" (Ferrell, 1997, p. 35). Leaving the small town of Marquette and coming to Detroit where there were many more African Americans and people of other diverse backgrounds, I begin to appreciate who I was and I did not have to feel like I had to work so hard to discern where people were coming from. I begin to have a better handle on what I wanted and who I was.

Although I enjoyed great success from Wayne, graduating with a 4.0, I was sad and felt alone because I knew I had to return to Marquette and the strained mentality of trying to work with people, who seemed for the most part not to want to be around me. I felt like I walked in two different worlds when I got back.

I tried to seek comfort from others, who were themselves wounded and incapable of giving. I remember sharing with a friend how alone I felt at times and being told I needed more then prayer to rely on. I needed real people. During this struggle, I made poor choices and bad mistakes some, which were spiritually damaging. I am not being evasive by leaving out details. Identifying the actors involved, does not serve any purpose. To unmask those who helped me engage in this folly; does not force me to take responsibility for my actions. Not unlike the gladiator rings of long ago, focusing on strictly on what others did to me as an adult, serves no purpose other than ruthless and perverse voyeurism of gore and misdirected violence. Where is the valor in that? I had to learn to become brave. By brave, I mean facing fear and going into the situation and handling whatever I faced.

A long time ago, Aliquipiso, an Oneida maiden came to be known for her bravery. The Mingoes would come and raid the Oneida camps setting their log homes on fire, taking the women and girls, and killing the men and boys. One day Aliquipiso had a dream, which showed her how to defeat the Mingoes. The dream, she related to the council. In the dream the Oneida were hiding on a high cliff and the Mingoes go to the foot of the cliff where the Oneida showered them with boulders that killed them. Aliquipiso, after agreement with the council, left the village to be found by the Mingoes. The Mingoes tortured her with fire, even they marveled at how much pain she could withstand. Then, when it looked as if she were confessing she told them that she would lead them to the camp. The Mingoes warned if she betrayed them they would strike her down where she stood. She led them to the base of a sheer cliff and in a loud voice cried to the Oneidas that the enemies were there before she was struck down (Erdoes, R., & Ortiz, 1984).

When I came back to Marquette, I was truly struggling to find a place in this world as a whole person. I prayed for conversion. I never prayed so deeply in my life. I worked at a Home Health Agency as a Medical Social Worker. After which, I was offered a job as a Counselor. I was at a good place in my professional career having secured a job as a Counselor at a small, private college. I was in good physical condition, optimal weight and all that. I was working a hundred miles away from my boys in the Keweenaw Peninsula and in the winter that meant seeing them seldom, I kept an efficiency apartment, unless I wanted to risk life and limb. I really was not sure how to make it all work. I made the adjustment though it did not come to me in a dream as with Aliquipiso. I would become self-sacrificing more my friends, my family, and my community. I made that mental adjustment to really be sincere in my work. This took bravery, every day I traveled away from my family I had to wrestle with emotions and why I was doing my work. But I made the adjustment. However, after two and one-half years, of commuting back and forth to Marquette from Hancock Michigan to only see my family on the weekends I was called to make another adjustment.

On one of my weekend visits, getting friendly with my husband, we produced another baby boy. I had a reason to move home that outweighed the benefits of work. I do not think that I would have ever given that job up without the arrival of my third son on the scene. Yes, I was using family planning. You might say well maybe I was just careless. I think God intervened when I was in need and could not seem to see a way to change my circumstances so that my family could be reunited on a full-time basis. As much as having that money to assist with bills was important to my family, being there to raise them has been very important to me. I hope that I help them to grow up strong and well. People ask me a lot these days where do you work. I say that I work at home. It often comes to them as a shock that I truly am at home. My being a housewife does not define who I am, although I used to be defensive about it.

I used to feel that I had to make a point that I was working on my Ph.D. but I beginning to not care. I do not think we were made to all work 8:00 am to 5:00 p.m. and leave our children to the care of others; only to see our children for maybe a total of two hours a day except on weekends. Then turn around and do it all over again. If we see are children on that schedule, we are spending approximately 26 hours with them. But what else might we be doing in that time that is not engaging our kids, cooking, cleaning, shopping, visiting friends, going out, etc. Then how much time is truly spent with the children.

I always saw myself as a good provider, but I should have qualified that as being a financial provider. I will admit that when I came home on a weekend, I would make the sacrifice, hard though it was, to play with my kids rather that do a load of clothes right then. To be with my children has always brought me my greatest joy.

In this chapter, I went from developing my own social cognition through school, living in a different environment, taking risks, and making mistakes. I learned to interact and develop affinity for a variety of people but not until I started to appreciate who I was in the world. I will close this chapter with a poem because change has to start our minds.

> I overlooked the real
> Joy of life and what it should mean
> There's so many ones
> Unfortunate not to see
> What we've seen
> I made a promise to myself
> To keep my joy
> And to stop giving it to someone else
> Not to let negative people
> Change me or my heart
> Looking in the mirror
> Is how I get my start
> Misery loves company
> Why should I be unhappy
> Because of you
> I've looked myself in the mirror
> And so should you. (Watkins, 1999)

Chapter 5

EVALUATION

Mufaro had two beautiful daughters, Nyasha and Manyara. Although both were beautiful, Manyara was vain and had an unsettled heart. Nyasha was giving and compassionate. Manyara, because of her inner feelings behaved badly around others and mistreated them. Nyasha, had a nurturing spirit, which was symbolized by her abundant garden and ability to communicate with the forest animals, especially Nyoka the garden snake. A king asked of the villagers where Mufaro lived if any worthy young girls may become his wife. Mufaro offered that his two daughters go. Mufaro was innocent of Manyara's behavior, which she was careful to hide from her father. Mufaro arranged for both daughters to go the following day to the great city where the King lived. Manyara, determined to be queen, set out on the path at nightfall and was exposed to three tests. She meets a little boy, a woman, and a grove of trees. Manyare ignores the boy even though he says he is hungry, she yells at the old woman dismissing her advice not to laugh at the trees she has to pass through, and she laughs at the trees. Upon reaching the city, Manyara's glee turns to madness as she sees a five-headed monster upon the throne. Nyasha, makes it through the three trials approaching everyone and nature with reference. She gives the boy a sweet potato intended for her own lunch, the old woman a gift of sunflower seeds, and the trees on her passing seemed to bend down. When she reached the city, Nyasha was met by her sister Manyara and warned that marrying a monster would be her fate. However, when Nyasha entered the throne room she saw her little friend the garden snake. Who later transformed into the King. The King explained that he had been all of the figures that she had passed in the forest and asked for her hand in marriage as he felt she was the most beautiful and worthy daughter in the land. She agreed and his family immediately welcomed her and they were wed amidst much ceremony. Manyara became her slave.

As a child, I would have seen this story as an important lesson that teaches it is better to give than receive. As an adult, I know that if we are not superficial as is Manyara, our outcome in life might be better. Her superficiality is depicted on the cover of the book when she gazes lovingly into a mirror at herself. When we behave this way to the expense of all others, even ignoring warning signs of the impending danger this may cause, we may venture into madness. If, like Nyasha, we have an open heart, a willingness to give and be compassionate and nurturing, we may just survive intact. We will be able to focus on our inner life and the strengths within us, which others may see as weakness, but allow us to venture in the world with a freedom that allows us to see beauty where others only see ugliness born out of their own selfish natures. Included in this way of see the world through loving eyes, we also are able to look at ourselves through positive action.

I begin to become introspective when I became pregnant with my first child. This time of pregnancy, at least initially, was a time of peace. The year was 1987. The five years prior to my pregnancy were marred with turmoil. A number of things happened seemingly in union with one another.

When I first met the man I was to marry, we dated for a total of six months. During that period of dating, I was dealing with an ex-boyfriend who continued to stalk me. My grandmother had diabetes, which was making her very ill, ill enough to require hospitalization twice within that six-month period. As a consequence of my grandmother's illness, my twelve-year-old youngest brother came to live with Mark and me on a permanent basis. When my brother came to live with us, Mark and I had decided to move in together because we loved each other and because of finances as well. I don't know if I was ready to get married. I still was hungry for self-worth, identity, and meaning, things oppressed people hunger for (West, 1994). As I mentioned before, I desired spiritual sustenance.

Mark did not want to live with me. I believe even then he wanted to get married. I admit now that I was afraid to get married even though he was the only one I saw, the only one I wanted to be with, the only man I cared to give my heart too. I was afraid of the commitment and I was also afraid to trust for fear that at some point down the line I might be hurt again.

Mark has been raised Catholic. His mother strongly disapproved of our living together. We had pressure from her and my grandmother to marry. I did not think it was a good situation in which to help take care of my brother but I just could not seem to make myself take the next step and commit my life to Mark.

Aside from that was the tension of trying to find tenants to rent my grandmother's apartment. She had to eat properly and take medicine and it was costly. She also had hospital bills to pay and doctor's appointments. Back then the elderly did not have as many resources for help as they do now. She did have a house with one side that was converted into an apartment with a shared bath. The apartment was her asset, if she could find someone to rent it to.

To help my grandmother augment her income augment after my uncle and I moved out, I thought it would be helpful to find her some reliable tenants for her apartment. I worked with a company that could screen tenants and collect rent for a percentage of the money. The percentage of the rent that the company kept was high, about 60%. But the company did the background checks on tenants and collected the rent. All the landlord had to do was provide adequate space. I was disappointed when the plans came to an abrupt halt.

By the time I gathered all the information together and made the appropriate contacts, my grandmother had two guys living in her home. She told me that they promised to buy the house with their GI bill. When Mark and I met these two guys, I immediately did not trust them. They may have been brothers, as they said, but they did not even look like related at all. That's what struck me at first, how different from one another they looked. They talked a lot and they talked fast.

I tried to take my grandmother aside to talk to her privately and that also was impossible with these two guys. I am not one to hint and was very adamant about wanting to speak with my grandmother alone. I was about as subtle as a rock and tactful as a sledgehammer.

Those guys would not budge.

My grandmother would not either.

I asked here to reconsider this situation. She had no lease with them. She refused to ever look at any of the information that I brought over from the tenant organization.

I left mad. She was mad. I decided to just let things be. I had done what I could.

My grandmother had a verbal contract with them. Aside from her being an older adult, I respected my grandmother if not her opinion. But I could not tolerate the circumstances.

I was angry with my grandmother for her decision and I cut ties with her for a time. I was selfish. I did not call or drop by. Then, I got an urgent call from my uncle after a few months. He called to tell me that my grandmother, his mom, was again hospitalized. My uncle urged me to see what condition my grandmother's house was in. Upon following up on my uncle's call, I found the house in terrible shape. Garbage reached up to the ceiling. Dog feces were everywhere. The house reeked of rotting food, mold, unwashed bodies, and cigarette smoke. The tub looked like the inside of a used flowerpot. It was black with dirt as if someone had used it to grow something in.

My anger, grief, and guilt at being unresponsive to my grandmother helped me fight back the bile that kept rising in my throat. It threatened to choke me. My little Chihuahua was gaunt and malnourished. I went out back and my larger dog, King, was dead. I could not lift him. Mark and I put King in a bag and we hauled him off to the humane society. That is when my tears started to come. I felt irresponsible having left my brother and animals in the care of my grandmother. The men she had living in her house had ransacked it looking for the deed to the house. I was again confronting head on what I had been dealing with all of my life, "the lived experience of coping with a horrifying meaninglessness, hopelessness, and (most important) lovelessness" (West, 1994, p. 23). These men had no other plan than to try to take something that my grandfather and grandmother had worked for. For these men victimization had bred a sense of entitlement and they acted, in my opinion, as if everyone owed them because they had been victims of poor circumstances. I understand why they behaved the way they did but I did not condone their behavior. They had alternatives and like me they may have had to start life from scratch, working through their problems. To say, I can't get anywhere so I am going to take what someone else has got is wrong, period. But I cannot completely blame them, I intentionally broke contact with my grandmother. She may not have entered into any contract with those men had I been there to be relied upon.

As a consequence, I felt irresponsible having left my brother and animals in the care of my grandmother. The men she had living in her house hand ransacked it looking for the deed to the house, which apparently my uncle had it. I do not know when or how he obtained the document nor do I care. His lack of attention to his mother and her circumstances is what astounded me. I had to plead with him to take her. My uncle lived in Florida so he had some distance to travel to Illinois where his mother, my grandmother, lived.

Mark, still my boyfriend at the time, agreed to help me clean up the house so that if could be sold. I thought when Mark would see the house's condition he would surely leave me. He had "put up" [in my mind] with trying to care for my mentally ill mother until we could obtain hospitalization and treatment for her, my teenage brother who was agree and aggressive, and now the state of my grandmother's house.

Mark agreed. One of the men when asked to leave, left voluntarily. The other threatened to do me bodily harm and Mark went to call the police. They came and because the man threatened assault, they had him arrested.

We then went about cleaning the house. Waves of nausea hit me every time that I went in. I never asked how Mark felt and he never once complained. Sixteen 30-gallon leaf bags later, we could finally see the flooring. I mopped and scrubbed.

The tub looked beyond hope but standing water and bleach soaked the first layer of dirt away. I scraped and scrubbed to bring out the shine of the porcelain again.

My uncle came and got my grandmother. My uncle also managed to sell the house to a young family. He never talked about compensating us or anything us or anything. The next time I heard from him was to tell me that my grandmother had an accident, almost four months later.

After getting the house cleaned, things settled down for Mark and me. Not soon after that, Mark proposed to me. We had been living together for three years and caring for my brother. It was tough going financially.

I got laid off and bought a computer and started a home-based business and took a half-time job at the YMCA. I also cleaned apartments for our landlord. But even in tough times, nothing could erase the beauty of the day that Mark proposed.

Mark asked me to marry him at Crystal Lake Park. We would go there after to eat lunch. We occasionally will still go to the park here in Marquette off of Lake Superior. These trips to the park are among my cherished memories of our marriage. But nothing compares to that initial moment's specialness. We sat in our blue Ford Mustang. We painted it blue and I had made blue seat covers for it. We sat in that care, with the sunlight filtering through the overhanging branches of the trees.

Mark's large blue eyes, always conveyed gentleness and sincerity, were especially powerful today as he proposed. In light of all that we had been through together, I thought this man either loves me or thought I was totally nuts. Either way my heart said, "This one's for me" and "yes" popped out of my mouth.

It rained the day that we got married by the justice of the peace. The clerk sent us to the wrong courthouse so by the time we went before the

Justice of the peace we were completely soaked. The Justice took one look at us and said, "You two really want to get married, don't you?" My wedding day was a mighty powerful day for me.

I saw that I had worth that day, and maybe for the first time. At least in Mark's eyes, I had enough worth for him to commit himself to me. I saw myself through someone else's eyes. At that point, I literally allowed my identity to be influenced by the strength and stability that I found in the present.

Whatever we two did together became more important than my past or whatever I did alone. But it was not until I became pregnant with my first child, though, that I began to have a realistic, authentic approach to my self-development.

Exactly six months into our marriage, I became pregnant. If there is such a thing as the—Madonna effect, I had it. I envisioned breastfeeding my little one and snuggling close to her. I dreamed of counting her little fingers and toes.

I begin wearing maternity tops almost instantly. I was delighted with my condition.

I had secured a job at a publication company that I had previously typed manuscripts for at my home business. Coming to work for them was a blessing and I was able to give up working at home. Although there were conveniences to working at home, I had provided a pick-up and delivery of papers service that was taking its toll not to mention a lot of gas. The job at the publication company meant that I did not have to travel around town.

Having had the position just about as long as my new marriage, I had made adjustments but they were positive. I was enjoying my life very much.

Then thinks begin to change. The company transferred me from my cubicle to the receptionist area. I enjoyed greeting the people but I missed the busyness of typing.

I had learned that if you have a new job you are better letting the pregnancy show gradually rather than telling everyone. I do not know whether it was my performance, my pregnancy, or my husband's coming to apply, or simply none of the above [these were just things that floated around in my head, but shortly after they transferred me to the receptionist job, I was fired. My supervisor said that "it is your fault." I was told this without being given any specific explanation.

I fought being laid off from on organization with the outcome of them saying that I was inconsistent on the phone. I did not have enough left in me to fight this one.

I went back to running my home-based business but I no longer had the publication company's account. I do not think the company is still in existence anyway so I was done no real disservice in the long run.

Struggling financially, facing rising rent, taking care of my teenage brother, and facing the prospect of caring for a baby was stressful. Still, I had enthusiasm as it seemed the one bright spot in what was a pretty dismal financial existence. I wish at the time I had a solid Christian foundation, friends, or family capable of supporting me.

Over the next four months, I attended prenatal appointments at the local clinic, tried to eat as nutritionally as our budget allowed. I learned to live on a shoestring. I continued to clean apartments. I stopped drinking period. Not even the glass of wine that doctors recommended for relaxation. The prospect of having my own child was so compelling to me.

Both Mark and I, in our early twenties, changed a lot of our behaviors when my brother came to live with us. For example, we were coming home at a consistent time. Having meals at regular times, attending my brother's school functions, meeting with teachers, etc., became a part of routine.

Mark and I had not had much time to develop ourselves as a couple. Yes, we lived together, but six months after we moved in together, my brother came to live with us on a permanent basis.

Now, we were pregnant. I was changing physically and emotionally, sometimes through conscious decisions through following a proper diet. Often though, I fell pray to my raging hormones.

I also begin to change mentally. I became more introspective. Having had enough psychology courses to create worry, I begin considering the importance of infant attachment.

I would hold my stomach and contemplate whether I would be a good mother or not. Or whether, I like my mother might lapse into madness and be unable to care for him or her. Or worse, I would be physically abusive.

These thoughts appalled me and I would strain with determination against them. I turned to positive actions and thoughts. I focused on the things that I could do to ensure the baby's health: dieting, exercise, routine checkups, nutritional supplements and quiet meditation.

I don't want to paint a pretty picture of this time. I often had fits of rage. I felt out of control at times. I attributed part of them to the pill, which I had taken in the ten years prior to my becoming pregnant. The doctors tried to adjust the level of dosage and that just seem to make things worse. I had headaches and my hair fell out.

I talked with my husband Mark, and we both decided enough is enough. So I stopped taking the pill. I still had fits of rage though.

I had a choice, this was coming out because I was angry and scared. I also had a poor self-image. I was angry because of how I was treated as a child. For eight years, I was brutalized, starved, and locked-in. I did not know how to care adequately for myself mentally. The ups and downs that I felt, the doubts that I had about being a good mother, I still was not even sure that I whether or not I made a good wife.

Rather than rely on courage, strength, and my own personal resources when things got tough, I tried to use anger to control others.

At the time, I did not understand all of this. I only knew that my emotions could affect the baby and I would try very hard to stay calm.

I found dealing with my then teenage brother to be difficult. We moved into a duplex to accommodate him. I tried to get help with him but because we were informal guardians, our resources were limited. We all decided that when it was time for him to go off to college that he fill our forms to become an Emancipated Minor in order to be eligible for Federal and State assistance. [But that's another story].

During my pregnancy, Dwayne would run off. He got held up once by knifepoint. I wanted him to settle down with school. I guess because it was a place that had brought me the most solace even though I got into fights at school it was not everyday. I never knew what would happen at home next, I knew something would happen, and the something would be bad. At school, it seemed like had the promise of something. I would love any form of attention and when a teacher would smile at me, I would soak it in like a plant does sunshine.

Our financial circumstances got worse. Mark's fellowship ran out and he was unable to complete his work. I felt guilty about his not being able to get through his Ph.D. program. I blamed myself and my family circumstances.

For Mark, his work had been a source of his identity. He had worked hard for very little reward and now he had not more financial support for his studies. I imagine he dealt with feelings of valuelessness, a loss of purpose, and the fear of what might happen next. With a pregnant wife, dependent brother-in-law coupled with less finances and facing an uncertain future, I imagine that he felt paralyzed. On top of that, add my use of anger to try and control the situation, and I am sure that I fueled bitterness and resentment in my husband's heart.

Our social circumstances were challenged as well. Mark may have taken my need to use anger to control as blame, as a consequence, he withdrew from me. He looked for work and he tried to hang in there with school. I worked making less money than before. I felt tired and irritable most of the time.

Then one day I felt a soft tugging inside me. After that I started bleeding. We went to the clinic and the clinicians told me that I was probably miscarrying.

I did not want to hear that. The baby still showed on the sonogram. They said that I could go on bed rest for two weeks.

Knowing that we could ill afford my resting, I did my best to stay still when I could and put my feet up or lie down. This was not easy.

I was still dealing with my brother running off and that meant searching for him on foot. We all argued at times too. So even when I rested, it was uneasy and fitful.

When I went back to the clinic nothing showed on the sonogram and I was heart broken. I remember weeping uncontrollably. The day I went to the clinic people were protesting outside because it also was an abortion clinic. I remember being yelled at. They had no idea that I went for prenatal services and wanted with every fiber of my being to hang on to my baby. Mark and I had loved that little person into existence and I cared for it with my breath and blood. That baby was a part of our lives. I talked to my belly. I valued that baby even though I was never to hold her or see her face. The relationship between Mark and I grew stronger with the promise of having her. When I saw the baby was no more on the sonogram, I felt that I might as well not exist either.

I sat there. One clinician recommended that I talk to their grief counselor. I went into this tiny little room and the woman pulled out a pamphlet on grief. She laid it in front of me.

I just looked at her. She talked and I could hear her, see her mouth moving up and down, but I could not understand what she was saying. It was as if my grief had enclosed me like a bubble. She asked me how far along I was and I told her "four months" and she told me "Oh, you don't need this pamphlet then." She then removed the pamphlet from in front of me and ushered me out of her little room.

I continued to cry. I cried until I had great gasps coming up and out of me.

They took me to sit in a lounger. I was in so much grief, I don't even remember to this day what Mark did at the clinic. Later, when we returned home we broke the news to a few family members and friends that we had shared the news with.

We called his mother that evening with the news, we also explained our financial circumstances, and the challenges we had with my brother. It was as if the baby's death (miscarriage), had opened up the gates of both Mark and my emotions. Before this, we had been caught up in doing what we could to hold us together as a family unit, Mark, my brother, and I.

I went back to the clinic for a follow-up visit. When we were told that I had not miscarried all the way, that I had a "missed abortion" have and needed "a procedure," I felt sick and grieved all over again. Mark's mom helped us out financially.

Mark's mom sent us money and being frugal, we decided I would have the procedure done at the clinic. The doctor charged "only $50.00 dollars." We could use the rest of the money for food. They used the same procedure that they used with a D & C (dilatation and curettage). I wanted my husband with me and I wanted to leave at the same time.

As the procedure was being done, my legs shook uncontrollably. I felt disoriented. One of the nurses told me that was part of the flight or fight syndrome but I had to stay so that they could remove everything. The clinicians were perfunctory and quick. They discussed very little and afterwards, I was asked to sit out in the recovery room. I rested the appropriate time. Mark and I left in silence.

For the next several days, our financial circumstances went from bad to worse. I found that I just could not get up out of bed. I did not eat. I did not go anywhere. I just walked around in my bathrobe. I felt ashamed, ugly, and condemned. I felt maybe something I had done made me unsuitable for motherhood. Mark rarely talked to me and not at all about losing the baby. He was going through pain too.

I was aware of his pain. I was aware but I could not shake the depression that I was in I walked and reacted as if I was in a pit I could not climb out of. I would sleep endlessly and yet still be tired. My closest friend had moved to Chicago and she called when she could. She told me that if there was anything that she could do she would try and help. Only what she said to me had any significance to me.

Other family and friends said things like "just get over it," "you will have other babies," "with everything else going on, it was probably for the best," "something must have been wrong with it," or "it was not viable." What did I care about viable or not?

All of these platitudes and rationalizations, fell on me like rain on a hot stone. I didn't care.

I walked in a daze. I didn't smile or laugh. I felt as if my legs were mired in mud. I was a victim of "tyrannical emotional domination" from my abusive boyfriend (Drakeford & Drakeford, 1980). Although in reference to husbands and wives, Drakeford and Drakeford describe this as "'functional' or 'psychogenic,' implying the emotions have affected the bodily functioning" (p. 61). The Drakefords also talk about the opposite: "the influence of the body on the emotions" (p. 61). I am sure that I experienced both.

Action helped me survive the crushing grief that I felt. I survived deep depression without medication. I had to help my husband and my brother. I think when they looked toward me and sincerely needed help, that their talking and involvement with me is what pulled me out of my despondency. But I was far from Emancipated.

Looking with hope to the future, I begin considering options. In our situation it was becoming clear that we would likely take Mark's mom's offer to help us, which meant moving. I was moving into a realm where the man is in charge. Not only in the personal domain of my husband's home; but also in this small town where, as Wolff (1957) describes, would be entering an "interesting and obscure masculine complex which has had so much influence upon the woman's movement; that deep-seated desire, no so much that she shall be inferior as that he shall be superior" (p. 57). I did not mind giving up my prominent role in the family as far as finances were concerned, if it did not mean that I had to lose my respect and worth.

The positive outcome of my adjustment that I made in moving to Marquette, was that my individual diversity deepened as a consequence of how I compared myself to others in this community. I was able to discern similarities and dissimilarities with other people. Because of my previous experience growing up and my ability to survive, I had a great deal of satisfaction of who I was in my own skin. My estimation about my racial identification, gender identification, status and attraction, personality and obedience, sexuality, and values are an outcome of the crosses (descansos) in my life. All the experiences, the descansos, along the way were building up my identity. Those descansos developed my character to match what challenges were coming up.

Chapter 6

CULTIVATION

An African Tale: A chief had a beautiful daughter, named Tusi. Far and wide every, she was known by many in other villages. Soon it was time for her to be married and the chief had his warriors go out and still cattle for a bride price as his daughter had loved walking amongst the cattle with him in their own village. The warriors go to steal the cattle from a distant village. Surprised to see it not guarded by anyone, they trotted off with the cattle. They did not know that the cattle were guarded by a monster so enormous that on one end it was winter and on the other spring. He had forests and mountains on his back. When the warriors saw him they were not stopped and took the cattle anyway. The next day Tusi woke up to find the monster waiting at the gate for her. Scared, she went with him too afraid to do otherwise. She rode on his back and the monster took her to a cave which had corn growing in front of it. He demanded that she pick the corn for him. One time, she spied a man hopping through the woods and peering out of the edge of the cave. She placed her two hands on the mouth of the cave for balance. She discovered why the man hopped because he was a half man who had half of everything. He had spied her hands and rushed back to his village to tell them that there were two people in the caves. Returning with the chief, he demanded that the two people come out. Tusi came out. The chief and the man were surprised to see that she had two of everything and was quite beautiful. The man took her as his wife and fed her so much until she became very fat. The villagers decided to eat her. While they were carrying her, she called to the sky to save her. It thundered and lightening and the pot shattered. The men decided not to give anything to her to eat to starve her. She was glad to not have anything to eat and when she had lost enough weight to walk, she returned to her village and slept out in the open when she had to. Soon, she got back to her village and her reputation was as before and many chiefs from other villagers sought her hand. Her father, satisfied with her safe return, did not ever want her to leave. A chief asked his wise man to help him and the wise man devised a plan. He turned himself into a frog and asked the chief's daughter to follow him. As he walked with her, he also admired her beauty and changed himself back into a man and said you will marry me instead of the chief. Not wishing to marry the old man, she said head open up and everything she carried she placed inside her head. Her head was so misshapen that he did not want to have anything to do with her and so he led her to his village to the chief. When the chief saw her he said take her away but his sisters implored him to keep her. So, he did and Tusi asked her head to open up and removed everything that was in it. Tusi and the chief lived happily together (Arnott, 1962).

    Although I was not ransom for a monster like Tusi, I learned the hard way how monstrous financial debt can be. I felt responsible for our financial situation. I know that it did not help that I had that lag time in there after losing the baby when I did not get myself out to work. I chose, like Tusi, the best alternative at the time, which was to accept help from Mark's mom.

    After struggling financially for months, Mark and I came to accept his Mom's help. Accepting help from my mother-in-law, meant we had to move to Marquette, Michigan. I didn't feel welcomed here. Like Tusi and the village of half people, I stood out. It was not just my skin color, my personality seemed bolder against the background of most of the people here who seemed more reserved. I respect their difference as I do mine but it was hard to make the adjustment to here at first.

    Mark's mom was nice enough but I did not know anyone. Mark's Mom started receiving nasty phone calls. A person called and asked if a famous "black person" had moved in. My mother-in-law did not complain though and I have the feeling if I had not been there for that call she would not have said anything about it. She worked hard to keep us encouraged. I felt somewhat lost having gotten rid of most of my things. What I owned held sentimental value.

    We sold things off to use the money for the move. One thing I sold was a vanity that I had painted black and then painted flowers on top. The white flowers that I painted stood out thickly, I wanted them to have a lot of definition, and then I highlighted them with metallic copper and bronze petals and stems. I don't know why that piece was meaningful except it was the one thing I created after the loss of the baby.

I bought it for ten dollars and sold it for twenty-five. I sold off and gave away my houseplants. I had forty houseplants. I guess that I was nurturing even then. My friend who had been kind to me after the miscarriage, years before said my pillows and plants indicated that I was a nurturing person.

We let the Goodwill take a lot of stuff away. Even though I felt melancholy about leaving, the feeling was associated with giving up my independence. Otherwise, when I left I felt that I was leaving behind very few ties with family members. My cousins, who have proved genuine and supportive over the years, were the only ones that I had close contact with.

Also years before, my friendships that had blossomed in a college town, either became pen pals, phone pals, or the relationships died with the passage of time. Later my one good friend became an Email pal. Over long distance though, my friendships lacked the luster and depth that they once had with good old face-to-face human contact.

When I came here, I regretted my decision from the start. I came to find work and what I had done so easily in Champaign, word processing, not to have the demand it had in my hometown. I was not having success with it here. My strongest desire at this point was to earn money as quickly as possible to pay for my keep.

Mark went back with my brother and stayed with him until he finished his fall semester of high school, then Mark and my brother joined me up here in Mark's mother's house.

My days consisted of getting up, going to look for work, and coming back to my mother-in-laws house. Then, at my mother-in-law's house, I got a call from my Uncle telling me that my grandmother was in the hospital. He told me that while walking she had been hit by a car.

When I called the hospital, I was told that my grandmother had to have a leg removed. If she lives, I was told, that she may have to have the other one removed. She was in critical condition and they were not encouraging. My grandmother had been a beautician and she loved to walk. Her legs had always been sturdy. I remember her holding my little brother and looked at how strong her legs were. My great-grandmother lived to be 87 and I knew that my grandmother would live that long if not longer. But I suppose as a child, we think all of our elders are invulnerable.

My mind flashed back to right before we left to move up to Marquette. My grandmother called one time begging to be with me. She begged me to take her in. That was when I found out that my older uncle had placed her with the abusive uncle. We were not in any position to take her in. As my grandmother talked to me, I struggled with all the promises that I had made to her when she had become my legal guardian. I had promised to take care of her forever, even, to get her a new house.

However, my reality was that, we, ourselves needed caring for. In moving, I did not know if our fragile, new marriage would stand the added strain of living with my mother-in-law. She turned out to be kind, generous, and long-suffering. However, the social atmosphere was different here than from Champaign-Urbana. The number of African Americans or any other distinct cultural group was a lot less in this community. I had been used to making friends with a variety of people, male and female, and it was hard to get acquainted with people.

We were making slow gains from our money pit. I started working and paid bills as well as I could. I also gave to Mark's mom for food. I felt like I was taking advantage but she said that she was glad to help us and I believed her. I would have liked to have had a handle on my social situation, which proved more challenging.

People seemed reticent and provincial here, and primarily Caucasian. They hung out primarily with their families and friends that they grew up with. This was a different way of living then I was used to. I was used to making acquaintances with strangers quick. I had an easy time striking up conversations with strangers.

In my youth, we went from town to town, first with my dad who was in the United States Air Force. Then, after my parents' divorce, my mom's mental illness kept her in constant motion. In the eight years, we remained in her care, we moved to Colorado, Chicago, Champaign, and Indiana. Within each city, we moved from house to house. And when we did not have a house to live in, we hung out at the train or bus station. In Chicago, we lived at the train station. What my mom did in Chicago was to walk the streets with us at night. Then, go to the station during the day. We washed up in the train station bathroom. I looked forward to the little soaps because they fit in my hand and smelled so nice. After weeks of living like this, my grandmother came and got us before the authorities picked us up.

As a consequence of all this moving around, I became adaptable to people. I longed to make friendships. I was wary, but open. I took people at face value and made my own judgments after. I don't know how I hung on to that much trust but I did. Maybe it was because most of the more difficult moments happened when I was a child. Anyway, I met people from all walks of life.

People that I encountered here, at least in town, seemed to have an ideal vision of the world and it did not stretch farther than the borders of the town. I am not judging them, how can you have any sense of the world if you have never traveled more than two feet from you own place. I tried to engage people in small talk and I tried to get along.

Looking back on my upbringing though, I was not raised with those types of social graces. I am still learning those as I get older. Not that I can't behave well-mannered, I find that people here are often circular in getting to what they want. I did to be direct and to the point, often without tact, like cannon ball fire.

It is now that I am learning to communicate prudently, after being here for more than fourteen years. Although, I have to be direct as that is my way, my style of communication. In the beginning, when I first moved here, my way of communicating was taken as my "having a chip on my shoulder."

I thought this is a crazy way to live. People were walking around holding all their emotions inside. I used to call them the walking wounded. People were hurting in nice inconspicuous ways. Now, I pray for them. I never judged them. You cannot know how to react differently to others unless you are open to learning and meeting new people. In trying to adjusting to Marquette, I felt was a heavy burden that took quite a bit of my energy.

I decided not to focus on what or how the people thought and signed up for school and through my self into a routine. I took a risk by signing up for school. I did not know whether I would have to take a lot more courses. I ended up doubling my majors to Psychology and Social Work. I completed that work in five-years.

Tusi took the risk to follow the wise man. She had to make some changes to her head along the way. Although my head changes were not quite as dramatic as hers, I was on a way to a new beginning.

Chapter 7

CONCLUSION

An African American Tale: There was a story passed around from one slave to another that once our people knew how to fly. An old man, named Toby, it was said knew the ancient African words. It was even rumored that some people did remember how to fly. One a day, as many other endless days, African American slaves were beaten for working to slow. One slave in particular, had a child upon her back, and the weight of him coupled with the stooping and bending under the hot sun made her know she could not go on. The Master told the Overseer to have her whipped. The Overseer ordered the Driver to crack his whip across her back which struck her child as well. He cried out loud as any child would which has been hurt. His mother, overwhelmed by his crying and unable to comfort him could not go on. She pleaded with old Toby to say the words that would help her fly. Sarah weakly stood and told Toby, "I must go soon." Sarah, starved, saddened by her babe's pitiful cries sat down. The Overseer spit the words "get up, you black cow." As the "Driver's whip snarled around Sarah's legs," her dress was torn, blood ran from her legs and she could not stand. She pleaded to Toby "now, Father!" Toby said it was time and he held his arms out to her saying, 'Kum . . . yali, Kum buba tambe.' She walked into the air with the baby in her arms until she was gone from sight. The angered Overseer could not catch her. The next day more slaves were falling from the heat. Toby as before, with outstretched arms, said the words that put all of them in flight. The Overseer hollered and pointed at Toby saying that he was the one saying "the magic words." The person who called himself "Master" came running and prepared to shoot him down and the driver was ready to whip him. Toby, just laughed. He asked them whether they knew who some of them were. He said "we are ones who fly." He stretched up his arms and said " . . . buba yali . . . buba tambe . . . ." Those that could fly, "flew away to Free-dom." People who had to remain pleaded with Toby to take them too. Not laughing or crying, Toby, the seer knew that they would have to take their chances running. He simply said "goodie-bye" and was gone (Hamilton, 1985).

Reading this simple folktale helped reawaken me to the harsh realities of the life my people have lived. This awakening took place deep inside me. In order to get in touch with that feeling now, I recommend for anyone to see the films: Amistad and Beloved. Ultimately too, this folktale prompted me to think of how two hundred years of slavery could be endured. If we have a collective unconscious as Jung suggests, then in answering one of the questions I put to myself, I say that we have to change ourselves as well as change our environment. I think back on my ancestors and many who could not run had to transform themselves through their imaginations, memories and stories to survive a brutal existence in which often a dog was treated better. Even kind treatment was not a match for freedom.

What does it truly mean to let things go? It means knowing that no one is righteous. It means that we truly need to focus on nurturing our spirit rather than the laws of man as God intended. I do not profess to be a theologian. To me, Toby represents the human spirit of the African American slave carried back as far as their ancestors. What gave us as a people the strength to endure the harsh realities of human law. The people who flew were the people whose hands may have been chained but deep down they knew another way. Toby had only to remind them how to be free, to fly. Free their spirits of this place.

I grew up doing the sixties and seventies. I remember when Martin Luther King spoke out for freedom. Reflecting upon this story, The People Could Fly, Reverend King knew how to fly and he knew how to teach others to fly with him. The story is symbolic of the courage it takes to do something that you are not accostumed to. For me, it is not merely running away; it is taking a stand before your enemies without becoming like them. It is an acknowledgment that you were not and never will be like them, 'we are the ones who fly."

To reflect on that ability to fly listen to Martin Luther King Jr's words in a letter from Birmingham Jail:

Just as Socrates felt that it was necessary to create a tension in the mind so that individuals could rise from the bondage of myths and half-truths to the unfettered realm of creative analysis and objective appraisal so must we see the need for nonviolent gadflies to create tension in society that will help men ise from the dark depths of prejudice and racism to the majestic heights of understanding and brotherhood.

King knew that freedom has more to do with self-mastery than merely dropping the chains that restrain physical liberty. When our spirit is not nourished our creative energy diminishes, we are distracted and in essence our mind does not work right.

We all ought to be able to fly than but we tend to avoid the tension Reverend King, Jr. invited. In my opinion, people do not want to think to hard or to deeply about the concerns of the past nor the global issues of today. In my own personal experience, I am compelled to do so.

The story also talks about loss, how people had forgotten the ancient words, the African Mystery. I felt deep personal sorrow when I read that because I think of how I have been truncated from my heritage. I would have liked to have known who my people were and how they lived. But I think that the pain and burden of their endurance made them not what to talk. I had an opportunity to do a case history of my grandmother and she declined at the last minute she did not wish to share who she was with anyone, they were "nothing special" to her. To me they were extraordinary. The little I got. It was like having "potlicker" left over and trying to sop it up with bread. The history of my family never was enough and left me wanting more. I have only my cousins now who know more about my family then I do. I sent some photos to them which they identified. I plan to send a genealogical chart. I find though that even though the genealogical chart can show relationships. It is like having a skeleton with no flesh. I want the stories, the people's stories and it may be too late. I hope not.

Maybe, if I had acted earlier with more reverence for my family earlier, I could have learned more about them. I wish that I had not let that part of how I came to be out of my grasp. I can remember sitting on my grandfather's knee and I know that there were stories. I can see me in pictures of my Dad, only having those to know what his face was like. I can remember my Dad taking me to visit his mom in Richmond, Virginia. I can remember her name but not her face.

By reading about other people's lived experiences, I felt encouraged to right about my own. Although mine is not as dramatic as Hill's (2000) who is trying to save the trees, or as socially relevant as Rose's (1990) who uses his expertise to encourage other's ability to write, or as awe-inspiring and courageous as McCourt's (1996) survival of extreme poverty. My perspective in this piece was to use writing as inquiry (Richardson, 1994) to become more truthful about aspects of my own life by reflecting on the harder experiences of my life to derive at different perspectives and learn new ways of coping. By rewriting my experiences, the exercise of writing itself becomes an expression of my hot cognitions (Brande, 2002). My hot cognitions and 'being' emotions helped me begin to convey how I developed through the "construct of expressive writing" (Brand, 2002, p. 2).

I am still learning the process of how to go about writing more creatively. I am learning the power of getting to know one's own self and how that knowledge can work not only to release emotional burden but help to provide impetus for positive change. Hopefully as a consequence, it may in some ways encourage others as an outcome. Other resources that I used on this journey, was a literary directory of African American writing (Magill, 1992), writer's handbooks (Brande, 1981; Burack, 1999), and of course writer's resource books (e.g., Craig & Hopper, 1996). The point in all of this too is to become a better writer through rewriting and reading others' work and continuing to rework my own work. To look not only at the mere recording of my life events, but using writing as a craft to sculpture the essence of those events in meaningful ways so that my 'narrative of self' (Richardson, 1994, 521) is revealing in ways that are useful to qualitatively explore the feeling states that surround the behaviors, physical events, and personal cognitions. It is a way to deal with the thorns on the branch of my life and it is only the beginning.

Aardema, V. (1995). Herstories: African American Folktales, Fairy Tales, and True Tales. New York: The Blue Sky Press.
Angelou, M. (1997). The heart of a woman. New York: Random House.
Brand, A. G. (2002). Hot cognition: Emotions and writing behavior. From JAC, University of South Florida at http://jac.gsu.edu/jac/6/Articles/1.htm
Arnott, K. (1962). African myths and legends. New York: Henry Z. Walck, Inc.
Backus, W., & Chapian, M. (2005). Telling yourself the truth. Minneapolis, MN: Bethany House Publishers.
Brande, D. (1981). Becoming a writer. New York: Penguin Putnam, Inc.
Burack, S. K. (Ed.) (1999). The writer's handbook. Boston: The writer, Inc.
Clark, K. B. (1963). Prejudice and your child. Middletown, CT: Wesleyan University Press.
Cline, F., & Fay, J. (1990). Parenting teens with love and logic. Colorado Springs, CO: NavPress.
Courlander, H. (1996). A treasury of African Folklore: The oral literature, traditions, myths, legends, epics, tales, recollections, wisdom, sayings, and humor of Africa. New York: Marlowe.
Craig, R. P., & Hopper, V. F. (1986). 1001 pitfalls in English Grammar. New York: Barron's Educational Series, Inc.
Drakeford, J. W., & Drakeford, R. (1980). Games husbands and wives play. Nashville, TN: Broadman Press.

Erdoes, R., & Ortiz, A. (1999). American Indian trickster tales: Myths and legends. New York: Penguin Books.

Guinier, L. (1998). Lift every voice: A new vision of civil rights and social justice. Keynote lecture of the Human Relations Series at Michigan Technological University, Houghton, Michigan.

Hamilton, V. (1985). The people could fly. New York: Random House.

Hooks, B. (1992). Black looks: race and representation. Boston, MA: South End Press.

Hill, J. B. (2000). The legacy of luna. San Francisco: Harper.

Lester, J. (1992). Black folktales illustrated by Tom Feelings. New York: Grove Press, 1992.

Magill, R. (Ed.) (1992). Masterpieces of African-American literature. New York: Harper Collins.

McCourt, F. (1996). Angela's ashes: A memoir. New York: Scribner.

Richardson, L. (1994). Writing: A method of inquiry. In N. K. Denzin & Y. S. Lincoln (Eds.), Handbook of Qualitative Research (pp. 516-527). Thousand Oaks, CA: Sage Publication.

Rose, M. (1990). Lives on the boundary. New York: Penguin Books.

Walter, M. P. (1985). Brother to the wind. New York: Lothrop, Lee & Shepard Books.

Rutstein, N. (1993). A Prescription for the disease: Healing racism in America. Springfield, MA: Whitcomb Publishing.

Serwadda, W. M. (1987). Songs and stories from Uganda. Dillon.Danbury, CT: World Music Press.